I was born a boy, from Venus

2nd edition

It's time to be yourself

Ella Marques

Coral Orchid Press
North Miami FL

I was born a boy, from Venus

I was born a boy, from Venus

Disclaimer

I have tried to recreate events, locales, and conversations from my memories of them, as well as I could. In order to maintain their anonymity, in some instances I have changed the names of individuals, companies, and places. I have also changed some identifying characteristics and details such as physical properties, occupations, and places of residence. Some dialogue is reproduced and can be seen as fiction.

© 2020 Ella Marques, "I was born a boy, from Venus" second edition

Cover design by Ella Marques

Graphics from IStock

Proofreading and technical support by Hatch Editorial Services. www.hatch-books.com
 Coral Orchid Press, Boca Raton, FL

Printed in the USA

ISBN: 978-0-9987029-6-4 Paperback
ISBN: 978-0-9987029-7-1 E-Book
 Visit us at: www.ellamarques.com

Contents

I was born a boy, from Venus

Introduction

Hi, my name is Ella Marques, and I am in the process of transitioning from a male to a female, at the age of sixty. I am an MTF transgender woman, meaning I was born a male but always knew that I was a girl, and now I am finalizing my journey to become my real self.

There are several reasons for me to write this book. One of them is that I would like to share my extraordinary life with the people I know and love, my family and close friends. Another is that I would like to inform those people with whom I do not have much contact about my transition. Finally, to show an example of what transgender people go through to all readers, whether they are transgender or not.

I was born a boy, from Venus

My life is not only extraordinary because I am transgender but because I am an international person who has lived in many countries and had very different experiences within them. Yes, my femininity has been the constant throughout my life, an inseparable part of me from a very young age. I tried to suppress it but never succeeded, and that is why I always ran away from myself, from country to country.

For my transgender community, I would like as well with this book to say that we are all very different but we have very similar stories, that there is a way to survive and to fight for what we are and feel, that there is hope for us, that we are finally being accepted in some parts of the world, but we still must fight to be free. Each one of us must choose our own life, but being real and free is something we owe ourselves. This gender feeling does not go away; it is part of you. As with all actions, the courage to face our biggest fears is the way to freedom and to real challenge. Look for help; there are a lot of great professionals for transgender people – like Dr. Carol Clark, whom I mention within this memoir – who can help you and support you. There are many support groups you can reach out to, locally or through the internet. There is a light at the end of the tunnel. Go for it, do not give up.

I was born a boy, from Venus

I would also like to tell non-transgender people that we can and do struggle through many years of suffering before we make a decision to be what we really are. Unless we are accepted from a young age. Why are we transgender? I think only God knows, and this is not the issue, this type of diversity has existed for thousands of years and will continue to exist in the future. But in this time of openness and acceptance we should learn to live and accept our diverse society. I always think about the transgender people that live in areas where they are murdered and persecuted. The other day I had a contact with a young girl in Afghanistan that wanted to commit suicide; she was lonely and afraid to live. Worldwide there still is a lot to do to achieve acceptance and freedom — not only for transgender people but for women, the LGBT community, racial and religious minorities as well, just to name a few.

For those I know and that have no clue that I am transgender, I would like to add that I am not alone. There are many like me. Please respect us and help us to be free. I'm sorry if I did not tell you, but I may have feared your reaction, the risk of losing my job, losing our friendship and your respect. Believe me when I say I needed a lot of real courage to take this step. Please embrace and respect it.

I was born a boy, from Venus

John Gray wrote a book called *Men are from Mars, Women are from Venus*. Well, Mr. Gray, I was one of many exceptions. I was born a boy, from Venus. Hence the title of this book.

To the most important people in my life: Karin, Victoria, Raphael, David, Gaby, Monika, my sisters Luisa, Ninita, and their fantastic large families, I would like to thank you for being so tolerant, for sharing your love and acceptance, and for being with me.

Last, I would like to thank my parents, who are both no longer with us, for doing the best for me. I miss you, and I am sure that somehow you would be proud of what I am doing.

For this second edition, I would like to add that many things changed in my life, thank you to all people that have been correct and fair with me, the list is very big to mention all of them here.

Transition means by definition a big change, for me change has been the only constant, sometimes more welcome than others. But change is as well progress and growth, things that I embrace and love. Read more about my transition on my second book "Coming home to Venus."

Finally Coming Home... to Venus

*"Three things cannot be hidden: The
sun, the moon and the truth."*

Buddha

It's Wednesday, early in the morning, and I, Ella, just woke up. My usual first thoughts:

"What are today's goals? Finish the exhibition, follow up on mailings from last week, go to the urologist, define next steps..."

I get up, do the usual routine. Go to restroom, step on the scale: weight is 165 pounds. This is stable, but I would like to lose another ten pounds and somehow the scale is going the wrong direction. Well, considering that just one year ago I was 200 pounds, this is not so bad. Shave, brush my teeth, shower, and put on my toiletry creams and liquids. Most importantly, the bust enlargement cream and the hair regrowth liquid.

Then returning to my room, I decide to do some work before I go out, so I put on panties and a bra with a V-neck T-shirt and hot pants. I like the V-neck T-shirts. They remind me just how much my breasts have grown.

Morning work, some e-mails sent to customers, two telephone conferences with Switzerland and Germany, the usual routine. I telephone more customers to keep them updated and to keep our friendships going.

My engineering company is progressing somewhat slowly, but it has been a source of great joy and freedom. I finally have some time for myself, my thoughts, and, most importantly, my feelings. Well, after sixty years of hard work, running away from myself, living in denial, and cross-dressing, I was ready to reboot my life.

When I say cross-dressing, I mean living as a man doing all male things because I had to. At the time that I am writing this book, I still must perform some tasks as a man. I have not told my customers and partners about my feelings or that I am a transgender woman. But things will change, and it is not something that you can do automatically. There are too many steps to perfection, when everything is legal.

I have a very precise roadmap as to when and how I am going to change. I have been taking some time to define the steps on my roadmap and to review it on a regular basis, this roadmap for my transition. I still have a lot of work to do, and I must earn money to live. I travel a lot for my business, and I must have my paperwork ready, that means with my new name and gender tag before I show up in a new location as a girl.

Living in South Florida near Fort Lauderdale, I am very privileged as a transgender woman because acceptance is strong here. I am part of various transgender support groups, and there are several highly qualified transgender-focused medical professionals, psychiatrists, psychologists, surgeons, and other forms of support, such as estheticians, electrolysis specialists, laser specialists, you name it. This is not the case all over the U.S., let alone around the world.

I think a lot about our community, especially trans people in North Carolina who were not allowed to go the bathroom of their choice because of the law some years ago. I even have some transgender friends who were turned away from a hotel in the same area in 2016. This is so insane. So many transgender women are beautiful and have nothing more that can be connected to the male gender. Can you imagine a transgender woman with a vagina being made to go to the men's bathroom? Or on the other hand, many trans men are very handsome and masculine, some highly muscled. If they were to go into the girls' bathroom, I am sure the girls inside would react very strongly to seeing one of them there. When you travel as much as I do, such things matter.

I cannot understand how people think that transgender people are "men dressed in women's clothes to look at or molest young girls in the restrooms." I heard this statement on the news, where it was explained as the basis for the "bathroom laws" in North Carolina. This is so ridiculous. Only criminals would do that, not transgender people, who simply need to have the basic rights to relieve their most basic needs in peace.

The transgender community is quite incredible. You meet some very special and intelligent people, some average, and some that face difficulties to make ends meet. From NASA engineers, airplane pilots, some incredible consultants and bankers, business owners, and lawyers, all the way to sex workers. But we cannot forget the people that have gone through hard times: the drug addicts, the people who suffer from severe depression, the people who are homeless, the ones who have tried to commit suicide, and especially the ones who did kill themselves or were harmed, aggressed, or even murdered by others. Unfortunately, rates of suicide and attempted suicide are very high with both trans women and trans men. I am talking about well over 40% of trans people here, of all genders. Certainly, a large reason is acceptance. It is not easy to accept yourself if society is against you, and it takes a lot of strength to overcome the pre-existing pressures we have to deal with, including that foundational one we were given from a young age, to be "normal."

In December 2016, the National Center for Transgender Equality, a leading U.S. transgender organization, published the 2015 Transgender Survey. All statistical values within this book are based on this survey. This survey was taken by 27,715 transgender people, and I was one of them.

My goal is clearly to have a body that is coherent with my mind and the way I feel. I made some incredible changes already, but I still have a long way to go to achieve what I am looking for. It will take a long time.

I was born a boy, from Venus

When I was fifty-eight, I lost my job. The company I was working for got into financial difficulties after many years of CEO changes and mismanagement. So they started to reduce people, and I was the first in line. This was probably one of the best things that could have happened to me. It took me out of my comfort zone and made me transition from employee to entrepreneur. It did not take me long to decide to work with companies that supported me and believed in me.

Just one snag: I had worked with teams of people my whole life, and suddenly I was alone. I had time to think, and even more challenging, I could feel again. Mainly I could feel how unhappy I was with my life. I was smoking two packs of cigarettes a day, and spent my time addicted to anything and everything.

I had to understand what was going on with me, so I looked for a professional counselor to help me. I understood that to live and be happy I had to find out and accept the way I am and the way I function. The first step was to understand myself and my feelings. After sixty years of pollution, it is not easy to distinguish what is the essential part of you and what was programmed into you by others: that is, family, friends, and society. This was not so easy for me because I came from another generation. I was born in the baby boom of the 1950s, into another civilization that I now have almost no contact with.

I was born in Portugal, and throughout my life, I experienced a multitude of cultures that left many traces on me, mainly the Portuguese, English, Swiss, French, and German cultures. I speak seven different languages, have lived in five different countries, and have visited even more. So I experienced a lot of confusion about the set ideas that I had to sort out. It took some months and a great therapist who specialized in sex and transgender issues to accomplish this. Dr. Carol Clark was an essential help for me to understand myself, mainly to understand that it is okay to have feelings, my *own* feelings, and to live accordingly.

The results were fantastic. I gave up smoking overnight with no help and issues, that is, cold turkey! No more addictions, and believe me, I had many, such as drinking, playing video games, and poker, among others. Well, I gained some weight but immediately went to a specialist and lost a lot of weight together with my lovely partner quite fast. We both look much more attractive now, a big, big difference.

Then some months later, the miracle started. I finally got my letter stating that I was suffering from something called Gender Dysphoria, and I started Hormone Replacement Therapy (HRT).

Wow, this was such a difference from the phytohormones I had before! I found peace with myself and with my environment. Now, I don't know how I could ever have lived without them.

The main goal of my transition is to achieve happiness and that means something regular and positive and in the sign of acceptance and love.

I had a spouse, Karin, and any change is always difficult, but going through a transition like this raises the stakes even higher. There are different stages in such a transition. In the beginning I still looked like I did when I got married, and acceptance and understanding was there. Once the transition included larger breasts, pronounced body curves, and other physical changes, then Karin's reactions certainly experienced a new attitude towards my transition.

"Your breasts are growing," Karin said one day. "This transition is getting more difficult for me."

"I am the same person as before," I replied. "Why do you feel this way?"

I was born a boy, from Venus

"I am not a lesbian. To touch your breasts is not something that is normal to me." She steeled herself and said, "I have to bury my husband before I can understand Ella."

"I understand you. let us work this out together," I said to Karin, and she showed a sign of agreement.

The effect of the hormones on your feelings, your appearance, and your sex life is quite large. Yes, feelings and estrogen are inseparable, in all you do, not just with your reactions when you are watching famous tearjerkers like *Titanic* or *Gone with the Wind*. With testosterone blockers, your amorous desires are just not there anymore, at least for a while, and dressing in the clothes of the gender that is the same as your spouse is not an issue if there are no competitive feelings between you, meaning not only who looks better.

Most marriages will crack under these new conditions, and I suppose I was lucky for a while, in that we had a lot of trust and decided to honestly try to stay together. It is challenging but worthwhile to do so if you have a good relationship. Well, I must clearly state that I have told Karin that I am transgender since the first day we met twenty-four years before, and trust is always based on honesty. We have a very deep love for each other, probably more platonic than physical now, and these are the basic facts of our relationship. We had a period in our time together when the physical attraction was very intense and beautiful and that helps us now to feel in this new level of partnership. Even with the good relationship that we have, we made compromises on both sides to try to get happiness, and it is a constant work with its ups and downs. These downs are mainly driven by two things: my sense of guilt because I am changing and her sense of fear because things are not the same anymore. Both of these feelings have no reason to exist and are wrong! It is a new phase in our life, and we must accept what we are and how we feel. It is a process of growing up. And let's face it, although I have changed a lot in the way I look, at my core I am still the same person, with the same values. In our case, in addition to my changes in gender, our daughter Victoria left our house to go to college and we became empty nesters, making things even more challenging.

The first person in my family I told about my transition beyond my spouse was my daughter, Victoria. One weekend I went to Tampa, where she attends college, and we went for dinner in a restaurant in the Ybor City, an old part of town. I wore my male clothes.

I was born a boy, from Venus

Jess, a dear friend of Victoria's and our former foster child, was with us. While she went to the restroom, I gathered all my courage and said, "Victoria, I have something very important to tell you."

"Okay," answered Victoria with a very inquisitive mind.

"Your father is going to change gender and become a woman." I finally got the news out.

"Wow, that is something new for me. How long have you known this?" asked Victoria.

"All my life, Victoria. When I was five years old, I was already getting dressed as a girl in my sister's clothes. I always tried to stop it, but I could not. It always came back to me, for the last fifty-five years," I said.

She sat back in her chair. "I would never have expected this, although I know you are not the most masculine of men. And what is your girl's name?"

"Manuela, but please call me Ella," I answered. "For a number of months, I have been treated by a therapist, Dr. Clark, and she has diagnosed me with something called Gender Dysphoria." I took out a copy of the diagnosis letter and gave it to

Victoria to read. "I have been taking hormone replacement therapy for some months already."

We could see that Jess was coming back, so Victoria told me, "Let's talk about this later, but I would like to tell you that I will always love you as my father, and the important thing is that you are happy."

She just showed me that there was a mixture of shock, understanding, and a limitless love. I will never forget it. She proved how fantastic and understanding she is, and confirmed this again as she gave me a Christmas present that was for Ella, the first one that Ella ever received.

Victoria is such a great girl and proved that love beats all barriers. Over time, she has proved to be one of my best supporters, confidantes, and advisors. She helped me immensely then and still now to gain self-confidence. Soon after, she asked me if she could tell her boyfriend about me being transgender. I said yes, though I also said we should decide together with her mother. She told him soon after, and again, there was acceptance.

Jess is a brilliant girl that was very close to our family, since she lived with us for one year as our foster child. I have a lot of admiration for her. She was literally left more or less alone by her parents who live in South America, and she is a great student and a very independent and intelligent person, a real survivor. I think that we are the closest thing to a real family for her. I will never forget that at a very young age, she was teaching English to Chinese students in China.

One day, after I'd told Victoria, Jess came to our house.

"Jess, I have some news for you. I am going to change my gender and become a woman." I told her.

"What? You mean you are transsexual?" she asked.

"Well we call it transgender now," I answered and added, "I have been feeling this way since my youth, but then, my family was very strict and did not accept it."

"So, you are doing like Caitlyn Jenner?" She had seen some episodes of the television show *I am Cait*.

"Yes, like Cait, at least almost." I then showed her some photos of Ella. "I will tell you everything over lunch, but first, please let me know if you are okay going to the restaurant with me, as my real self, as Manuela."

"Please do. I would love to go with your female self," answered Jess.

I went to my room, put on my makeup, dressed in a short skirt, a blouse, and some high heels. Then I put on my wig and went to the living room where she was.

"Wow, you look really good!" Jess said. Well, that is something a girl loves to hear, no difference with me now, a kind of balsam in your heart.

"Thank you. Let's get in the car to go to the Farmer's Table, and I will tell you everything," I said.

During lunch I explained my feelings to her, the changes I was going through, and my experiences. She was quite inquisitive and positive towards it; she was the third "family" member to learn about my transition.

The next people I told were my two sons, Raphael and David.

Raphael came to our house with his beautiful girlfriend Julia for a two-week holiday. They live near Zurich, Switzerland, so they don't come every day. I decided to have my sixtieth birthday party while they were in Florida; little did they know that it was also my one-year anniversary of hormone replacement therapy (HRT).

I was born a boy, from Venus

When I picked Raphael and Julia up from the airport and drove them home, I was wearing male clothes. We had a nice evening, and the next morning, I told Raphael.

"I would like to talk with you, Raphy. Can we do it in my office?" He followed me to my office, we sat down, and our conversation continued. "I have to inform you that I am going to change my gender." My heart was racing with nervousness and fear.

Raphael looked at me in an inquisitive manner and said, "Okay." There was a very puzzled pause and then he said, "What makes you take such a decision?"

"I have been like this all my life, that is, since the age of five," I said. I described what my feelings were and showed him the letter from my therapist.

"Wow, that means you have been suffering for fifty-five years!" he answered.

"Yes, my son, that is correct," I said.

"Let me see, now I have three mothers: my biological mother, your wife, and now you."

My heart was racing again, but this time out of joy. I could just feel what a fantastic person he is and his acceptance. The rest of his stay, I was Ella.

I was born a boy, from Venus

Some days later my oldest son, David, arrived for my sixtieth birthday, and I did the same thing.

"David, can you come to my office? I would like to talk with you," I told him.

We sat down in the office, and I told him.

The astonishment was clearly visible on his face. He was not exactly shocked but overwhelmed.

"Wow, how long have you known?" he asked, and in the same fashion, I told him the complete story. His reaction and feedback were fantastic. "I love you any way you present yourself, as a woman as well," he said.

In the end of the conversation, I asked him if I could tell his wife, Gaby.

"I would like to tell her myself. I wonder what her reaction will be," he said. That night we all went to a very nice restaurant to celebrate my sixtieth birthday and Ella's first birthday, that is, my rebirth after the start of Hormone Replacement Therapy. Except for Gaby, all of my family was there. I was wearing a nice black skirt, blouse, and black high heels, and I was the happiest girl in the world.

The next morning, Gaby sent a very long and lovely text to Ella stating that she understood me better now, and that acceptance and support were there. I was crying of joy and happiness; she will always be in my heart.

My daughter Victoria told all her friends as well that her father was going to become a girl, not with shame but with pride. One of her Swiss friends, Alessia, was in our house for two weeks and attended my birthday as well. She became a very dear friend of mine, full of understanding and a lot of fun. With all the girls, we went shopping together for makeup, clothes, shoes, and all girly things, and I went shopping with them as Ella. I must say, most of the salespeople were so nice to me, sometimes I received more support than my daughter. As a matter of fact, there is a makeup shop here that my daughter prefers to go with me because we get much better service when we go together.

The next big challenge was to tell my sisters and their families. I flew to Lisbon, Portugal, during a business trip to Europe. After dinner with one of my nephews, Luisa and her husband Joao drove me to their house, and we sat down in the living room. It was the right moment to tell them, and my heart was racing; I was really scared.

"Luisa, Joao," I began. "The reason that I came to Portugal is to give you some news. I.... am going to become a woman." There was a kind of silence and some surprised faces.

I carried on. "I had major depression, visited a therapist, and started HRT over one year ago." Luisa is a doctor, so she knew exactly what I was talking about.

She immediately interrupted: "That does not surprise me at all!" Well, Joao's face got even more inquisitive while she took a small pause. "I remember when you were five or six and you used to go through my drawers, take my clothes out, and dress in them." Joao looked even more surprised, but my sister carried on. "And I remember that our mother would punish you for it."

"Wow, you still remember that? I am really impressed," I said.

"As long as you are happy, that is the most important thing," she said.

I then stated, "During dinner we were talking about our mother's depression and how that was caused by taking DES (diethylstilbestrol) to prevent miscarriage while she was pregnant with me. Well, that affected me, too." DES was the first artificial estrogen, and I will write about this medicine in the next chapter.

I was born a boy, from Venus

We carried talking about our mother until Luisa asked, "What about Karin?"

"Karin has known that I am transgender since the first day I met her. Yes, twenty-five years ago I was extremely depressed because a psychiatrist refused to give me hormones, and that was just before I met Karin. There are no secrets between us."

Later when I went to bed, my heart was light, I had just dropped a stone, and I was feeling happy.

The next day, we went to the beach house some miles away from Lisbon, a place where we were raised, and where Luisa and Joao have a house now. Juana, Luisa's oldest daughter, her husband Tiago, and her two gorgeous boys were there, too. The last grandnephew was born just a couple of weeks before my trip there. Again, I told them and the reactions could not have been more positive and understanding. Juana wrote me a beautiful e-mail later on.

Tiago told me, "Uncle, we are very open-minded and understand you. It is important that you are happy."

Filipa, Luisa's second daughter, came to Luisa's house for dinner the following day. We were at the table, and suddenly Luisa nudged me very gently me with her elbow and whispered in my ear. "Are you going to tell them?" I said, "Sure," and then turned to my niece, Filipa.

"Well, your uncle is going to become your aunt." I saw some very confused faces, so I continued. "Yes, I am going to change gender and become a woman."

Filipa immediately said, "Like Caitlyn Jenner?" and I said "Yes." The reaction was positive, and I showed them some photos on my iPhone. "This is Ella, your aunt."

Filipa replied, "Oh my God, you look so nice! I am so happy for you. What about Karin? How is she dealing with it?"

"Karin has been a great support," I answered, "and we hope to stay together."

Every time that I opened up about my transition, I received a lot of questions. The first was always about my wife and how she felt about it. It proved to me how strong, understanding, thoughtful, and fantastic my family is. To go through such a transition with understanding and support is so important.

Transitioning is a long process. The goal is to live in the gender that your psyche knows is right, but unfortunately you were not born that way, so there are a lot of challenges to overcome. After all, you want to be at ease and be accepted for the way you look and behave, and I am doing this at the age I am. I am not trying to be a supermodel, just the sixty-year-old woman I am.

I live now as Ella in Florida, and I am very happy about it. I go shopping, to restaurants, and to every other public place as my real feminine self. The Swiss Club, where we have many friends, has been incredibly nice and open. Just recently we had Christmas dinner there, and Karin and I were two girls.

One of the members looked at me quite inquisitively, and I presented myself.

"Hi, I am Ella," I said.

"Okay, I am John," he answered. I was almost laughing because I noticed he did not recognize me.

"Remember me? I used to be Fernando, the president of the club."

"What! I did not recognize you. Fernando was not so handsome, but you look very pretty," he said.

We received so many compliments. Most of the people knew me as a man and now met me as a girl. I feel very privileged that my acceptance has been so wide and people have been so open. Until now I never had many issues with my transition, except when a certain local doctor refused me to give hormones.

Most of the issues I have experienced, which this memoir will explore, were driven by myself and my insecurity, not by my environment. One thing is very important when you are transitioning, and that is your level of self-confidence. In this case, it is more important than in other situations, and it has to come from within you. People – and I mean *all* people, not only transgender – accept others on the level of self-confidence they perceive. If the self-confidence level is high, it is easier to accept a person. Being transgender means that you are going through a drastic change, and in the beginning, you have to learn everything, so your self-confidence level is very low. It takes time and a great deal of courage to get there, but it makes you a better person.

In my case, there are many things to overcome. Throughout my life as a male, my body had a high level of testosterone, meaning the male evolution has been a very long one.

The earlier one transitions from male to female, the easier it is; it's preferable to transition before puberty, so that there is no damage from testosterone. Theoretically this should be possible, since a large number of transgender people know what they want before puberty. Similarly, for trans men, transitioning before puberty means that it is easier because they will be able to avoid breast growth and menstruation.

Implications of transitioning get worse with age, not only because of the physical appearance but also because of social implications. Family, children, and work are some key factors that must be taken into consideration. That said, we must never forget that the challenges for a transgender person are difficult at any age. Transitioning at puberty is very complex as well, with its own challenges. These can be difficult because in the dating world, the refusal of many people to accept us is a constant threat. Can you imagine? Many young girls have acceptance and self-confidence problems, and for transgender girls, it can be even worse because they have to fight for their bathroom rights in school, fight against bullying, and fight desperately to get normal friendships and relationships.

I am very lucky because at my age I still do not have extremely masculine features, such as my feet, which are a size that is quite common with women, so passing as a woman is not such an issue for me. Still, there is a long way to Nirvana, to become the girl I always felt I was. My plans to get there are quite clear now.

The hormonal change that I am undergoing will take two to three years because of my age. The chance that hormones will completely change my appearance are low, so thank God that surgery can work miracles.

FFS, or Facial Feminization Surgery, will make sure my face gets some of the basic feminine features. It includes a nice feminine nose, a hairline that looks like it was not destroyed by testosterone, a pointed chin, and more developed cheeks. In my case, I do not have many issues with the Adam's apple or other typical male features, but some trans women have theirs shaved down. There are a number of books available on the subject, and some highly specialized surgeons for this type of intervention.

Breast augmentation is, well, the dream of most if not all male to female transgender people. The question here is how big the implants should be. I am a believer that one should let the breasts grow naturally before making such a decision. Many transgender women do not want to wait, and they get large implants from the beginning, then they grow, and gravity has a strong effect on large breasts with time.

Unfortunately, many transgender girls do not have the money necessary for such treatments and so they inject themselves with silicon. Some organize so-called silicon parties. This can be extremely dangerous and has even killed some people. The butt is another region where silicon is injected, but in all cases, any kinds of fillers or Botox must be done by specialized doctors and in a proper way.

Several types of smaller and some not-so-small interventions are available, such as body contouring, liposuction, and tummy tuck.

Other interventions that must be taken into account are electrolysis and laser hair removal. Since most of my facial hairs are white, only electrolysis works. This is a long and painful process where an electrical current is put inside your pores using a needle, and the underlying hair is taken away. This must be done to every individual hair. Well, I have been doing this with a great lady, Lise Anne Jensen, and we became very good friends in the year and some change that I have undergone this treatment. The most important thing is that the person who treats you does not make scars or other type of imperfections to your skin, and Lise Anne is very good at avoiding that.

The ultimate goal for any transgender is SRS, Sex Reassignment Surgery, also called GCS, Gender Confirmation Surgery. This is a difficult and long surgery, and the number of doctors that have a lot of experience in this subject is not very high either. Since being transgender is now in a boom phase, many hospitals try to offer such surgeries, but many lack experience. In many countries, there are decent doctors, but in some Asian countries, there are real experts. Anyone considering this surgery should just be careful because not all doctors are good in those countries, and it can be a very dangerous experience in the wrong hands. Here, too, there is quite a lot of help and information available on the Internet.

Gender is in the mind, and sex is between the legs. In reality, these are two different things, and there is no obligation to undergo such surgeries to become a complete person. There are many stages of gender fluidity, and anyway, what is between your legs and how you use it is your own business.

For trans men, the challenges are completely different but certainly not easier. Testosterone changes your physical appearance and voice over time, making some trans men very handsome indeed. Still, some trans men suffer a lot with the special breast binders until they undergo removal surgery. Testosterone is a very powerful hormone and risks have to be well-considered.

FTM (female to male) gender confirmation surgery is quite a challenge, too. Here as well there are some doctors that can perform real miracles.

All interventions can be painful, risky, and costly and are not always covered by health insurance, although many things are changing. It is very important to decide how far to go, but only one person can decide and that is the patient.

Appearance is not the only thing that is important when you change. Paperwork is important, too, and sometimes a nightmare.

My own identification documents are rather complicated. I was born in Portugal, a country that since 2011 allows a name and gender change on one's birth certificate, pending confirmation from your therapist and your doctor. Switzerland is my second nationality, where things are even more complicated. If you are Swiss, to have a gender change on your papers, you must undergo both SRS surgery and divorce. Well, in my case, the Swiss authorities have to change my data because of my changed birth certificate. The next hurdle is that I live in the U.S., so I must update my paperwork here as well. That's three countries to get over with, each with their own issues, injustices, and understandings, and that is just to be able to get on a plane like a normal person and not like a weird piece of cattle. And of course, to be able to piss without having the fear of going to jail in many states in this country.

Changing papers in the U.S. is quite a jungle in and of itself because many different states have very different legislations. Again, the National Center for Transgender Equality (www.transequality.org) and the Human Rights Campaign (www.hrc.org) can be a great sources of help and information, especially in today's changing times.

The other most important roadblock for any transgender person, or any other person, is their financial situation. In my case, I have a transgender-owned company, a company that can use diversity guidelines. Transitioning is expensive, and on top of it, I must earn a living for me and my family. Survival is not always easy. I have been very lucky in that my parents left me a great inheritance. This was not in money, which I always earned myself, but in international experience. Until now, I always managed to cash in on this. I hope that will continue.

Acceptance by my customers and partners will certainly be an obstacle to overcome. I am working on it and have a plan for the transition, but this will mean that I must be very acceptable as a woman.

But the future is always in intimate connection with the past, with one's history. Why am I the way I am? Why do I think the way I do? What have I learned? Where am I going?

I was Born in a Golden Pram

*"There can be no keener revelation of
a society's soul than the way in which
it treats its children."*

Nelson Mandela

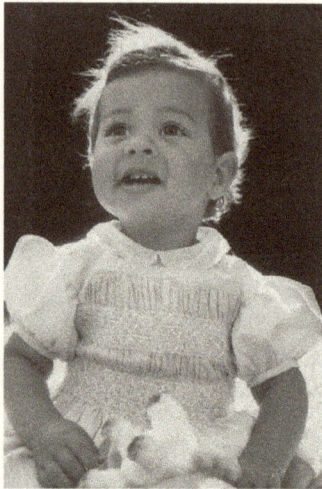

I was born in Lisbon, Portugal, in 1956, and I have witnessed how society has changed in the last sixty years for many countries and civilizations.

Can you imagine a life without television, or only black and white television? We did have a telephone, one that was made from black plastic, was hardwired, and at home. Communication was very different then: books were kings, people met to communicate, there was no Facebook, no mobile phones. Transgender and LGBT people more generally were jailed in most countries. Transgender people would be jailed for fraud because they were wearing "clothes from the other gender," and in some places, they would even have their heads shaved as punishment.

I was a baby boomer, according to Dr. Spock, the latest provider of ideas on child education and society. My family was not exempt from this general 1950s fad.

My mother was the daughter of a white Portuguese man from quite good families and a multiracial French-African mother. My grandfather divorced quite early, so my mother was sent from Africa to Portugal at a very early age, where she was brought up by her aunt, my grandfather's sister. She came from a quite well-known, upper-class family in Portugal; her father was a writer and landowner in Angola, Africa. He had the second-ever driver's license in Angola, which was a Portuguese colony at the time. (The governor had License No. 1.)

My grandfather was a fascinating man. He wrote many books about Africa, some copies that can be found in the British Museum in London. He was a lion hunter back in the 30's, and he had a beautiful Hispano-Suiza car, a very expensive car at that time.

Somehow in the early 50's, he was put on a list of people that wanted to revolt against the big dictator Salazar, so he was put in a political jail for some time and lost all his fortune. He then came back to Portugal and died just one year before I was born. My mother had an intense society life with her aunt in the north of Portugal, where her family held aristocratic titles, and she stayed a royalist all her life. She worked as a medical laboratory researcher in the Institute of Hygiene and Tropical Medicine before she met my father. This was quite unusual for the time, to have high society ladies working.

My father was the son of country folk. At the age of fourteen, he was sent to his uncle in Lisbon and started working. He was a clever, hardworking man and became quite wealthy. He had an incredible memory, and he could calculate sums in his head at incredible speeds. He was a charmer and had a good sense of humor, but he was not the easiest person to deal with. He sometimes had a difficult temper. He was not much at home either physically or mentally; he was always working.

My parents got married quite late for that time. My mother was a very thin, beautiful, multi-racial woman. She had four children: the oldest was a boy, then two girls, and I was the youngest. My brother had a difficult birth. They misused the clamps, which affected his brain so that he could neither hear nor speak. He died at the age of seven, the same year I was born.

My mother had a lot of psychological issues, and, as was typical at that time, the doctors gave her hormones while she was pregnant with me to lower the risk of miscarriage. At that time, it was a medicine known as DES (diethylstilbestrol), the first synthetic estrogen, making me a so-called "DES Son."

So-called DES sons have a tendency to become transgender or gay. There are other side effects that I can relate to such as stunted growth and non-cancerous cysts. This medicine was forbidden in the U.S. in 1971 for pregnant women, although it was still used in cattle. In other countries, this drug was used for many years. There is quite a lot of information about DES online. There is even a website called "DES Action" (www.desaction.org), which serves to inform people about its effects. Further information is available on http://www.antijen.org/transadvocate/id33.html.

As with most DES mothers, my mother suffered from depression after I was born. Her case was so bad that she had to be placed in a psychiatric clinic and finally sent to a secluded resort in Switzerland.

She dealt with depressive episodes most of her life and fought them with pills, which caused her to gain a lot of weight.

As a result of her treatments, I did not see my mother much when I was very young. I was brought up by my nanny with the help of my mother's aunt until the age of eight.

Nanny was in reality like my "mother"; she was always there for me. I liked her a lot. When she married and left, it was the end of the world for me. The picture of her leaving our summer house to get married is still in my mind today.

The first photographs of me show me wearing a dress. This was not so uncommon in those days because I had two sisters, so the youngest boy would wear their clothes. But already at the age of five, I knew that I wanted to be a girl. I remember very well that I had to share my room with one of my aunts, and once when I saw how she got dressed, I was fascinated by the process.

My two sisters and I were joined by my cousin, my father's sister's daughter, who was slightly older than my oldest sister. She had the nicest underwear, and since I knew that I wanted to be a girl, since I knew my mother and nanny would refuse me those clothes, even punish me for it I decided to rummage through her drawers and my sisters' to get their clothes. I borrowed bras, panties, dresses, and skirts from them. My mother and nanny would tell me:

"You are a boy, and boys don't cry!"

"Don't wear girls' clothes!"

"Don't play with dolls!"

I started to pray that God would make me a girl the next morning, but this did not happen either. Since I was not allowed to wear bras or panties in public, I decided to wear them underneath my pajamas and go to bed with them. I got caught all the time and was regularly punished for it. At that time it was a round of belting on my bum, or some other type of physical punishment.

As a young boy, before I began school, I was very creative both in drawing and storytelling. It was a great time for me: people accepted me and liked what I did. I was very thin, and to my mother's eyes, I was not growing as I should, so she took me to a doctor who prescribed me synthetic thyroid hormone and to a physical therapist to grow my lungs. I had a big, large belt around my chest that I had to train with. I hated that treatment.

My mother's idea was that I had to look like a boy. I was extremely thin for a boy, so I was given huge portions to eat to become stronger. Sometimes I was even force fed, so I would have hysterical attacks and throw myself to the floor and scream. (This was quite good because they would lock me in my room, where I could wear my girly clothes in peace.)

The first time I traveled was when I traveled as a small boy with my parents and sisters to Portugal's neighboring country, Spain. I do not recall everything, but I do remember that I was very pretty and always liked to follow my own rules, so at four years old, I decided to take off and discover the streets of a Spanish town called Badajoz, next to the Portuguese border. I made some very fast friends, but when my family found me some hours later, they were very angry with me. The people I met were apparently an American family, and they liked me so much that they asked my family if they could adopt me.

As punishment, on the next large family trip to Paris, I had to stay at home with my nanny, someone I hated, she snored every night so loud that I would wake up, and I was in the adjacent room. Later they took me on a one-month road trip to Spain, France, Italy, and Switzerland. It was a very nice trip, full of culture, especially in Italy where we went to some of the most iconic cities, like Florence, Rome, Milan, and Padua.

Being born a boy, I was supposed to play football and play with toy cars. I always got those things as presents, and when I was caught playing with my sisters' dolls, well, there was punishment again. Sometimes, they would lock me in the bathroom for hours, though I preferred to be locked in my room for the obvious reasons.

After my mother's depression, we got an apartment in Switzerland. I lived there for six months with her, just before primary school. This was my first international touch. During this time, I went to a kindergarten that taught in French. My mother tongue was Portuguese, so I did not understand much, but it was fun. At that age we all had very easy communication skills. The hands were very often better than the mouth.

I have a vivid memory of going alone from the apartment to the kindergarten in a *trottinette*, a two-wheeled kids' scooter. You had one foot on the scooter, and the other on the ground as propulsion instrument. Going alone to school in Switzerland at the age of seven is kind of normal. Our apartment was in Vevey, a very nice city on Lake Geneva. I remember playing in the lake harbor, where I was always impressed by the sailing boats. In Montreux, the next town over, there was a casino, and I used to go there with my mother on Sunday afternoons for a kind of kids' party. I remember as well a coffee shop in the center of Vevey that my mother liked a lot, and we went there regularly. There was a piano player there, and we would listen to the music while I admired his playing skills.

This time was quite exciting; it was the beginning of the 60's, and a new culture was emerging. Being in the French part of Switzerland, we were often confronted with French culture and some names that were iconic, well-known for that time. My idols were always women, and at that time, I was fascinated with Sylvie Vartan and Francoise Hardy. I wanted so much to look like them!

Back in Portugal, primary school and the first years of secondary school were a torture. I had to adapt, to follow the rules, and I had a very difficult time doing so. I was doing everything possible to evade and rebel since I could not be myself. I was mostly friends with girls, and I was always the outsider with the boys. Somehow I always had issues connecting with other boys. I had good friends, but always from a distance. I felt guilty because of my femininity, so I did not share my emotions with my friends. I was scared to share, to get caught and punished. One nice occurrence at that time was that my two sisters had a pajama party, and I wore a pair of their pajamas.

Luisa and Ninita, my two sisters were always very different. Ninita, the oldest, always had a very strong personality and wanted to be in the middle of everything. Luisa was a more closed person, but someone I could trust and do lots of mischievous things with. They were both beautiful girls and very well-groomed.

In primary school, I remember daydreaming a lot in class and not listening to the teacher. Somehow I still took reasonable notes, and all my teachers loved me. I was always a big talker. My mother made sure that we were occupied all the time. Outside of school I had piano lessons, then violin and guitar. On top of this, I always had a lot of private lessons for mathematics, physics, and other subjects. Through these, I met some very interesting people that shaped my life.

One person I will never forget was my piano teacher, Campos Coelho. He was a professor at the Lisbon Conservatory, a great piano player and photographer. My sisters and I were all pupils of this incredible person, and we were part of his annual concerts. Some of his students became world-famous piano players like Maria João Pires.

Our instructor was such an artist, and I really liked the creativity and knowledge he portrayed. I wanted to be creative. Piano playing brought me a great sense of discipline as well.

Music was a very important thing at home. Ninita was the best piano player, Luisa played piano and violoncello, and I played piano, violin, and guitar. I played violin until I went to boarding school and was killing the ears of all my colleagues with high-pitched, out-of-tune practice sessions, so I started focusing more on the guitar.

Another person I still have in my mind was my mother's opera teacher, Dona Elsa. My mother lost her voice when she was sick, and she went to an opera singer to recuperate it. Dona Elsa used to be an international opera singer and now gave lessons. She came from aristocratic families and was a real teacher for good taste and all that is classical and beautiful. She was someone that promoted and supported the arts in Portugal by organizing children's operas, where of course my sisters and I were always present as young artists. At eight years old, I played the cook in Mozart's opera, *Così fan tutte*, though I always dreamed of wearing the princess dresses that my sisters wore. Dona Elsa was part of a charity for poor, young pregnant girls, and my mother was on the board of directors for that charity, something that occupied her time.

My mother made sure we had a very classical upbringing and ballet, opera, and classical concerts were on the regular visit list. I loved to go to the ballet; I was always amazed by how beautiful and feminine the dances were. Both Luisa and Ninita were doing ballet, and I wanted to do it as well, but of course: "Ballet is not for you. It is for boys that are very effeminate and you are not like that, right?" This is what I had to hear from my mother on a regular basis.

The 60's were very good to my father. From farm boy to millionaire, he did it all. By the end of the decade, he was the largest wholesaler in Portugal. He even got national recognition from a chamber of commerce for it. I remember he had the monopoly on Portuguese-made batik T-shirts, and he used to trade them internationally by the metric ton.

At that time, I was really running away from myself. I had good friends, but it was hard to keep them in the long run. Still, some were very special in their own ways. I will not say any names, as I do not know if they want to be mentioned here. They certainly know who they are.

I never gave up my girl clothes and underwear. For many years, I had a small wardrobe hidden in my mother's walk-in closet. I would go to bed, wait until everyone was asleep, then get up and get dressed. Sometimes I would get caught and get punished. My mother and nanny were constantly telling me that what I was doing was wrong and that I had to stop. The more they told me that, the more I rebelled, continuously rebelled. I was putting "stink bombs" in the class at nine, smoking at eleven, doing things to make me a rebel. One of the places I really liked was our family's farm, Carvoeiro. I always managed to disappear in the wild forest alone in my undies. It was a bit of a touch to myself and my nature that I never forgot.

One day, I had just purchased some stink bombs when my mother took me to a concert in Estoril, a very nice city not far from Lisbon. Well, these stink bombs consisted of a very thin glass sphere with a foul-smelling liquid inside. I put them inside a paper bag in the pocket of my coat. As we were leaving the concert, there were many people going out at the same time, and there was too much pressure on one of the bombs. It broke inside my coat so that I was really stinking. My mother was very distressed, and I was punished again. When I was in state school, around age ten, I was caught putting stink bombs in the class, and it was written in my school records.

At that point, my mother could not handle it anymore, so I was sent to a Catholic school run by the Jesuits, that is, until they did not want me anymore, and I had to go. I hated that school. I felt I was continuously controlled by people that were not as honest as they wanted others to believe they were. I always felt that the rules were for others, not for themselves. There were Catholic priests that had their own kids, some were gay, and many were very cruel. I always thought that religion was about love, not control over others, and yet the priests had some very sadistic ways of punishing us. By far the most painful was when they knocked on a pupil's head with the pointed part of a pen or pencil. Some of us would bleed. Another was when they would beat us on the hands with a wooden stick that had five holes. It was painful until we found out that if we rubbed oil on our hands the pain was not so bad. Please note that in those days, physical punishment was very common. The use of belts was another classic type of physical punishment, which my father used as well. My mother would use the hairbrush to hit me – not so nice either.

I was born a boy, from Venus

I was part of the Boy Scouts and in the youth group of a very special Catholic church called Opus Dei. It was a very interesting initiation into a lot of things under the umbrella of friendship and religion. The group was not really my thing, although we certainly had some very exciting activities such as speleology, the study of caves, which was sometimes very scary. We would explore incredibly beautiful caves, most of them in the wilderness.

I had many Jewish friends and felt quite at home at the synagogue. My mother always pushed us to follow the Christian religion, but the older I got, the less I came to terms with it. In the beginning, I really liked church. I was going there all the time, and for a while, I even wanted to become a priest. But I understood that there was a large gap between what they preached and what they do. Today it is even worse; they have not managed to change with the times, mostly together with their own followers. I always believed in God, I still pray every day, but the Catholic religion is something I gave up long ago.

The end of the 60's were for me an awakening to music, friends, parties, and of course, cigarettes and alcohol. My first cigarette came from the younger of my two sisters, and it took me a very long time to stop smoking. The music at the time was: the Beatles, the Doors, the Rolling Stones, Donovan, and so many other cult artists. It was probably one of the most enriching times in my life.

By the time I hit puberty, I was going through a very difficult time. I was getting even more rebellious, I had suicidal tendencies, and life was emotionally very difficult. Since my parents did not know what to do with me and my feelings, the next step was to go to boarding school.

"Fernando, you have to learn about discipline, and I don't know how to take care of you anymore. Your father and I have decided to send you boarding school, which is much more disciplined than here at home. So either you go to a Jesuit boarding school in Portugal, or to a Swiss boarding school. What do you choose?" my mother asked me.

"Okay, send me to Switzerland," was my answer.

Well, she didn't leave me much of a choice. The very idea of Catholic boarding school was a total disaster.

Boarding School in Switzerland

"Nothing endures but change"

Heraclitus

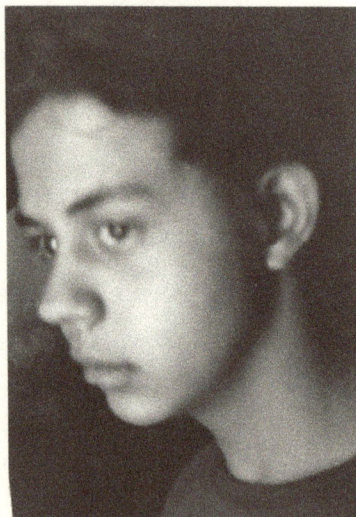

I felt very unlucky to learn that Le Rosey, the boarding school I would attend in Switzerland, had not had never had a Portuguese student, and that was since it started in 1880. This is one of the world's most expensive and renowned schools for the children of the rich and famous. It is mainly attended by the kids of aristocrats, movie stars, and millionaires.

My parents drove me to the school from Lisbon, and I was there two days before term started. I was taken to my room, where I spent the first night alone. Though I was a fourteen years old boy, was I scared!

The next day most of the other kids arrived at the school. I observed how old friends came together after the holidays. Only some of the new students, like me, had no one to lean on. Then I noticed something else: nobody could understand me, and I could not understand anybody. My mother tongue was Portuguese, and I was the only person to speak this language among the over three hundred students there. My colleagues came from all over the world, and the school taught its curriculum in French and English. I was put on the French track.

The first six months at Le Rosey were very difficult for me, and the reasons are many. For one, I had to suppress my feminine side and show how much of a man I was. No girly clothes allowed—not even my panties. The second was the language barrier. It was fun and I loved to communicate, but I spoke in a language that nobody understood. The third was the culture. I could not understand the customs of my colleagues; they were quite different from mine and I hated it.

I shared my first room at Le Rosey with two American boys who spoke French extremely well.

I was born a boy, from Venus

They had been in the school for a while and were honestly trying to be nice to me. One Saturday they went to the center of the town of Rolle, and as usual they smuggled something to eat into our room.

"Do you want to come with us to the supermarket?" V asked. I did not understand, but I think that was what he asked me. I moved my head positively and followed my friends to the store. First time I was in one; at home we had servants that did our shopping.

While we were there, they asked me a lot of things, but I did not really understand them. They bought quite a lot of food that I did not recognize, and we went back to our room. There we sat down on the beds, and my roommates started to spread mayonnaise on toast and distribute the food.

"Wait for the salami, it is very good," my friend told me, or at least that is what I think he said. Since I did not understand him, I started to eat the bread with mayonnaise and did not wait for the salami.

I am not sure if he then said, "I told you to wait for the salami!" or "Are you dumb or what?" It was probably both.

I was born a boy, from Venus

My only success was in math. I was very good, the best in the class. Within six months I had mastered French, and I started to understand my colleagues and their way of life, to slowly appreciate and embrace it. Then, from French, I began to learn English, and I started to become the international person I am today.

Even when my French and English started to get better, there were sometimes misunderstandings. Once, on a skiing day in winter, a girl told me that her birthday was in September. I replied, "Oh, you are a Virgin," instead of saying "You are a Virgo." She was very shocked, and I didn't know what I did wrong at the time.

Le Rosey is a very uncommon school. In reality, it is a secondary boarding school, but not like any other. It had and still has great teachers who coached us very well and professionally. We worked a lot, and there was a sense of academic competition that was quite incredible.

The kids who attend this school come from all over the world: France, the U.S., Italy, the UK, Japan, the Middle East... Sixty-five different nationalities, from every developed country and many underdeveloped ones as well. There were all religions, Catholics, Muslims, Jews, but most of them had something in common: they came from very elite families. Many of the parents had a very intense social or business life and did not have much time for their kids. This created a kind of family dynamic among the students, a bond that is still very strong today.

Le Rosey organizes fantastic activities for its students and has an amazingly international alumni association. I go to regular alumni dinners in many cities around the world. I have many strong friendships that were made over forty-six years ago and are still very active. I kept my feminine side secret all my life, so none of my school friends know about it as I am writing this book. It will be quite a surprise for them, I believe.

One of the great things about Le Rosey was the amount of sports we did. Well, sport was never my great love. When on the soccer pitch, or what the Europeans call football, I did not really play fair; I was the champion of stepping on the heels of my opponents. But in this great school, I learned to play tennis, basketball, to ski, to row, and my favorite, to swim. These were just some of the sports that we could do there. Every day we had two hours of sports and gymnastics, and in winter we had one whole day off of class for a skiing excursion.

Skiing was a very cool experience. I was so mad then because I was learning to ski in the beautiful city of Gstaad, in the Swiss Alps, and there were all these young kids that learned to ski literally before they could walk, so they were really good. I was fourteen, whereas they were eight or nine. Well, I finally managed to ski quite decently and to enjoy it.

During the winters in Gstaad, we always had our skiing excursions on Thursdays. It was the day that we went to the most beautiful slopes in Switzerland, and we skied the whole day long. We skied in places like Les Diablerets, over glaciers. We went to some of the most beautiful slopes in the Bern Oberland region, but also to places near Luzern, Matterhorn, Jungfraujoch, and others. I started to love nature, and much later this love was transferred from the mountains into the sea.

My best performance was with swimming, and in my second year at Le Rosey, I was on the swimming team. It was a lot of work and competition was not my strong suit, but I did what I could with it.

For me, my femininity at Le Rosey was replaced by an Oscar-winning role as a macho man, well, as good as I could perform it. The only thing that could be viewed as more feminine were my preferred trousers. They were these bell bottom trousers that were very fashionable in the early 70's, even for guys. I loved them because they somehow gave me a feeling of femininity and creativity.

The denial of my femininity, together with all the changes that I had endured, left its traces in the beginning of the third term of my first year at Le Rosey, when I suddenly had a pain in my left ear.

I went to the infirmary, and the nurse gave me some medicine for a cold. The pain did not go away, and within one week, the left side of my face was completely paralyzed. Cold medicine was not enough, and I had to do a lot of tests and go to a hospital in Lausanne. Some of these exams were quite extreme. One the doctors tested the reaction of my nerves by giving me increasingly stronger electrical shocks and measuring some kind of electrical signal with a needle stuck in a nerve. He took hours doing this; torture is probably the best description for it. All this torture to tell me that my paralysis was caused by an infection of the facial nerve that was in turn caused by an ear infection.

The doctors resolved the infection, but the cure for the paralysis took much longer, something like eight months. Over the summer holidays in Portugal, I had to go three times a week to the military hospital for my therapy. They dabbed the paralyzed area with a cream made out of stinging nettle plants, then massaged my face, and finally gave me an ice pack to cool down the pain. This was not a pleasure, believe me. For the first three months, I could not close my left eye, and I had to apply artificial tears so that it would not dry out and so that I would not be in pain. Back at school in Switzerland, all got better and I started to have normal functions, even if they were not as good as before.

Thank God I had two ladies that helped me emotionally: the late Mademoiselle Keller, the quite old, but in my case very supportive nurse, and the late Madame Schaub, one of the directors of the school. They were both very supportive and helpful.

This was not the case of all my teachers. One of the first days that I was paralyzed, after I left the infirmary, I went to math class, as usual.

"Fernando, where have you been all this time?" asked my math teacher. "It has been some two weeks that you have not attended class."

I got up, as was usual and expected for a student to reply to a teacher, and answered him. "I was in the infirmary and the hospital." Half of my face was paralyzed and only half of my lips were working, making a strange appearance.

"Ha, ha, ha!" He started laughing and pointing at me. "You look so funny!" He was laughing so hard that he had to leave the room to compose himself. I must say that he was the only one to laugh, and nobody in the class shared his emotions.

I had this freak feeling, and I started to cry. I was fourteen, and his actions hurt me, all my life long. For some reason, I associated this feeling with my transgender emotions, and it gave me a lot of distress, all the time. The president of the school recognized the situation, and this teacher had to leave the school.

Many of my colleagues had a lot of compassion for me and gave me moral support, partly because word of this incident spread throughout the school.

I have so many memories of trips, events, and people at Le Rosey, that I could write a book only about this period of my life. Many of the friends that I made then are still very close friends now.

Once a year, this school held a special orientation game that took place all over Switzerland. It was like a treasure hunt, except the region was a complete country. Children between the ages of thirteen and seventeen years old took the train alone, found hotels, and were responsible for their own food and drinks. It was challenging and gave us a great sense of orientation and organization. Switzerland is probably one of the only countries in the world where such a game can be played with young kids without the fear of kidnapping or any other type of violence.

"*Consigne, depreviligie.*" These were the two types of penalties you would be assigned if your grades were not good enough or if you did something that was not allowed. In both cases, you had to do an extra study session, and in the worst case, you could not leave the school on certain days of the week.

I had such penalties many times, mainly because I did not understand much in the beginning of the school year. My grades were lousy, so I had to do extra amounts of work. Our school had great stories about rule breaking that led to these penalties, and I played a part in some of them. Sometimes it was a pillow fight in the dorms or because we short-sheeted another student's bed. One of the worst things we did was to put one bed, including the student sleeping in it, in the swimming pool.

Another of my specialties was making electrical switchboards that were wired to the doors, so that we could listen to music and watch television with the door closed. When the door opened, the current was interrupted, so everything stopped working. This way, when our teachers came to control the situation, they could not see anything wrong or out of place.

Once in winter, our very rebellious class decided to prank our French teacher, the late Mr. Vuillmier. We took two cooked snails that we had bought in the supermarket and placed one on his chair, the other on his desk.

He arrived at the class with his usual rhythm. We were all sitting down with very serious faces. He entered the room, walked towards the desk, then threw his briefcase to the desk. It was a perfect hit, his bag landed exactly on top of the snail. Some of the kids in the class were almost cracking up with laughter, and that put the teacher on high alert. He took his hanky to clean the chair and saw the cooked animal. He removed it from the chair, then lifted his briefcase and found the second snail. He was furious. Immediately he asked, "Who is responsible for this?" No reaction from us whatsoever, just a lot of poker faces.

He got even more nervous and repeated his question, this time screaming, "Who did this?!"

Then the whole class stood up in one unanimous motion. We were all *depreviligie* for a while, but we never forgot it. We were a bunch of revolutionaries, and we loved it.

While I was in Switzerland, my sister Luisa attended a school in England called Hatchlands. The school was in a beautiful house owned by the National Trust with an incredible history. Some years ago, one of the courtiers of the queen, and his wife, who I believe was a nanny to Prince Charles, had a school for young ladies from very good families. Both my sisters were there at different times. I was invited to spend Easter holidays with my sister, yes, in the all-girls school.

The place was as stiff as you can imagine from English aristocracy, but it had its charms. First the house itself was exceptional; I believe it is now a park and a museum. Dinner was very English, as far as food was concerned, but I was among the girls. On Saturday, we rode from Guilford to London on the train. There a group of girls including two very good friends of Luisa, from the north of Portugal and another from Brazil. I was sitting with this group of Portuguese-speaking people. Another woman sat not far away from us.

"What a horrible woman," commented one of the girls in Portuguese.

"Did you see her makeup?" said another. "Way too much, it doesn't look nice at all."

"She looks like a terrible woman," said another, all in Portuguese.

"Girls, be careful. She could understand what you are saying," said one of the group.

"Forget it, she does not understand us," one of the critics said.

The rest of the trip was quite interesting as well because the girls offered me a copy of *Playboy*, telling me, "You can use this to dream about girls, but not about us. We are out of reach for you."

Well when we finally left the train in London, the woman that we had been talking about looked at us and said in the best of Portuguese, "Have a nice day, girls."

She obviously understood everything. The girls all got hysterical, laughing and screaming. We had some very fun times in England, and I loved to see Luisa.

I had a great time at Le Rosey in Switzerland, but after two school years, my parents called it a day, and I had to go back to Portugal.

I was born a boy, from Venus

This school was not only a great place than, but it is still one of the leading schools of the world. The association of the old students is very active and throughout the years has represented like a family to me, today many of my friends went to this school, even if not at the same time as me.

When I left the school, I had a real crisis, thinking that I probably would not see most of these people ever again.

Reflect on the good things I'd learned, Le Rosey taught me just how diverse this world is, about its cultures, languages, and religions.

All the same, it was the first time I experienced a feeling of loss, and it was hard for me to take it.

A Carnation Revolution

*"When dictatorship is a fact,
revolution becomes a right."*

Victor Hugo

Back home, the first thing I did was of course to go back to my old routines of dressing up at night. But this was a very changing and striking time for me. Too many factors were at play in my mind and body.

I was going through puberty, literally swimming in guilt because of the contrast between my gender identity and my changing body. In addition to this, there were major changes in my social environment thanks to a political revolution.

I was born a boy, from Venus

It was a ticking time bomb, so I decided to stifle my feelings in order to survive. I was a perfect macho male on the outside, but I was crying on the inside. I was very aware of what I felt, and I was gathering all the information I could get. It was a time when I also started to play poker, drink alcohol, and smoke like a steam locomotive.

And yet it all started nice and slow, picking up speed and strength, until I could not escape the growing avalanche.

In the summer of 1973, my parents sent me and my sisters on a month-long Atlantic cruise. It was a great experience, with new countries and new places to see: the beautiful islands of Azores, Madeira, the Bahamas, and Bermuda. We saw the famous cliff divers in Acapulco and the anthropological museum in Mexico City, and, for the first time in my life, I set foot in the country I would adopt much later, the American state of Florida.

For me, this trip was my introduction to boats, and sailing is still a great love of mine. It was the first time that I was in Cape Canaveral and Orlando, that I went to Walt Disney World.

It was a fantastic trip not only for what I saw, but for what I experienced. There were many parties and a lot of alcohol (sometimes too much), but there are two things I will never forget. One was that my oldest sister gave me some makeup for a costume party during the Atlantic crossing. I had girls' clothes on, but I was not the only one dressed in a female disguise. There was even a party guest dressed in a costume that was half-man, half-woman! One of the guests was a really nice girl. I could not stop looking at her and praying to be like her one day.

On the same trip, I experienced another "first" in New Orleans. On Bourbon Street, I went to a strip club, and there was a gorgeous girl with a male penis. I was quite impressed, not sexually, but with the idea; I had not known this existed. Another incredible experience I had on this trip was that, during a dancing contest, I won a bottle of whisky and drank it as well. I was taken to my room by two very beautiful girls that undressed me and put me to bed. The big issue is that I do not remember anything that happened that night.

Coming back to reality, I had a very hard year at school, because I had stayed abroad for a long time and had to take my Portuguese exams in 1973. I had missed a lot of the Portuguese classes and had to catch up. I was good at math and languages – except Portuguese, ironically – but things like history and biology were not my strong points. At the same time, I was trying to have a nice social life, meaning I had a very high level of absences from school. I was searching for something, for ideas, for myself.

There was only one way to succeed in my exams. For three months before the test, I literally closed myself in my room and studied from early in the morning to late at night. It was incredibly hard work. In the end, and to the astonishment of my teachers, I got very good grades, even in history, and my family was really proud of me.

I had already started to drive at the age of fourteen, and when I came back to Portugal, we had a family chauffeur. Due to her depression, my mother was a dangerous driver, which is why my father had hired the chauffeur. He also took me and my sisters to school and would pick us up in the afternoons. Well, in my case, I was usually driving, and he was in the front passenger seat. It was highly illegal, but at that time a kind of gentlemen's delight. Luckily I never got caught, but the principals of my school complained many times to my parents that students as young as I was were not allowed to drive.

During the summer holidays, I was often with my parents and sisters in Carvoeiro, our country house. It was a beautiful place where I could lose myself in the impressive nature.

One day at Carvoeiro, my mother asked me to get fresh water from the fountain for her.

 "Can I have the car keys?" I asked.

"Ask your father," she said.

"Father, Mother asked me to get some water from the fountain. Can I have the keys?" I asked him.

"Take them, but be careful. You don't have to win the race today, Fernando," my father said.

Well, that was that. I had the keys to the car, and I was ready for a joy ride. It was a very heavy French car, with a strong motor, so naturally I took it out on the dirt roads and drove like a lunatic. I made some very fast turns, kicking up clouds of dust behind me.

I was feeling confident about my driving skills. I had no idea why my parents were so concerned. I'd never had an accident, and I never would. I decided I'd had my fun and would now drive to the fountain to get my mother's water.

The fountain was in a kind of small geographical deflation, and as I approached at a tremendous speed, the car skidded in the curve and just went into that hole. I was okay, but try as I might, I could not get the car out of there.

"Shit! What am I going to do?" I thought.

I got out of the car and climbed back to the road. I was in agony looking at my father's car inside this hole.

"I will have to tell him, he is going to be furious with me."

Just as I was thinking this, I saw a man and his mule traveling along the road. I walked over to him and asked for help.

"I had an accident, and the car fell into this hole," I said. "Can you help me get the car out of there?"

He laughed. "Does your father know about this?"

I looked down and, ashamed, I answered. "Not really."

"Okay, let's go and tell him, then." He then took me on top of the mule, and we trotted home.

My father was waiting for me at the door when I arrived. I will never forget his face, staring at me with his mouth wide open.

"Well, you leave in the nice car and come back on a mule. What's going on?" he said.

I just looked at the floor. I couldn't get words past the feeling of guilt that was stuck in my throat.

"Your son was driving like a racecar driver and put your car in the hole of the fountain," the country person explained. "I can take it out with the cart, but I need your permission, in case of damage."

"Do we have any alternative?"

"No" was the answer.

The farmer hitched two mules together, and with the team, we were able to pull the car out of the hole. There were some minor problems but nothing extreme, thank God. My father was not very happy with me, and I became the butt of a family joke after that. "Don't be like your brother. Bring the car back and in one piece." I heard my father tell my sisters this for many years.

These were the last of the truly innocent days of my childhood. The Estado Novo would soon make sure of that.

April 25, 1974 was a very unusual day for me and for all Portuguese people, a day that utterly changed our lives. We woke up to find that there were no people on the streets. Military cars drove by, telling us from their loudspeakers to stay indoors. We turned on the television and radio. There was only military and revolutionary music on all of the channels, punctuated only by instructions to stay indoors.

We were very scared. We did not know how long we would have to stay inside, and we were afraid of running out of food, so we decided to see if we could sneak out to the supermarket that was next to our house. When we got there, we found out we were not the only ones with this worry, and there was not much to buy anymore. Most of the shelves were empty.

In the early afternoon, we heard from the television that a military coup had taken place and that they were going to replace the existing government. In the history books, this is known as the Carnation Revolution because that afternoon, all of Portugal was out in the street, giving carnations to the military personnel. That day, hardly any shots were fired. The problems came later, but not on that day.

The old Portuguese government was not very well-loved. The Portuguese dictator Salazar had run the country for thirty-eight years and died in 1970, some years before the revolution. He was followed by Marcelo Caetano, another dictator, the one who was overturned.

Until the revolution, Portugal was run very brutally. We had a political police called PIDE, and we were fighting many wars in Africa. Most families had at least one member that had died in these colonial wars; our family was no exception, one of our cousins died in action in Angola. The violence in the colonies had started thirteen years before the revolution; the government was a dictatorship; there was a lot of poverty. The Portuguese people had enough of this, and when the military coup happened, we rose up to meet them.

In 1972, two years before the Carnation Revolution, I went to a concert for Procol Harum, an English rock group, in Estoril, a very nice city near Lisbon on the shore of the Tajo River. All the kids were waiting outside of the park where this performance was supposed to take place. I was there with my sisters and some friends. My parents took us there and were waiting near Estoril's casino. All of a sudden, the place was full of policemen armed with shields and rattles. Some had dogs as well.

"Get out of here, run for your life!" We heard warnings from all over the place, and people ran in all directions.

The local office of tourism was not far from where we stood. It was already full, but my sister's boyfriend said, "Let's go there, we should be protected." We ran inside the building, which was already full of people trying to hide from the police. We stood close to the windows to see what was going on.

It was a disaster. The police started to hit the kids who remained outside with rattles and water hoses. Some kids picked up paving stones and threw them at the police. The police were beating the kids up, and we could see some of them bleeding and screaming. I will never forget this horrible scene. It was a good example of the old dictator's regime, and on that April day in 1974, we were glad to be rid of them.

The year 1974 was the year of the Carnation Revolution and the year of my own internal revolution as well. I had no choice but to play the male role, so I played an extreme one within the revolution.

Coming from a country that was a dictatorship, I had no sense of politics. There was an opposition party before the revolution, but it was not very strong. I knew that I was not a socialist or a communist, but I was not sure of the difference between the parties. I started with the extreme rightwing parties of Portugal. Then, as I got more informed, I moved to join the Central Democrats. I was a political activist, a defender of some of the parties, and in the evenings, a very well-known part of the night club scene.

At the time, Portugal was in total anarchy. The police were not there, and there were fights between the right and leftwing parties. One of my first parties was a very violent and extreme rightwing organization. We were very dangerous, throwing Molotov cocktails at army cars. Some of us would ride horses into schools and wreak havoc and destruction with axes and catapults. Every day we drank a lot, partied a lot, and had sex with as many girls as possible. It was important to show one's manhood, or at least in my case, to try to.

In the evenings we would put political posters up in the streets of Portugal. We always traveled in groups: two were on the lookout for the enemy; at least one was driving and looking for a secure place for a fast get-away; the others were gluing posters on the walls. Sometimes the communists would come at us with baseball bats and start a fight. We fought sometimes, and sometimes we would run for our lives; it depended on how many there were on each side. If we didn't have posters, we would spray paint the walls with graffiti. The streets of Lisbon and all over Portugal became an ugly warzone of political propaganda.

I was born a boy, from Venus

One day our political party decided to throw a big, big social gathering. Being the rightwing, we somehow thought it would be a nice idea to have swastika decorations. Every time I think about this, it makes me sick. We were kids and did not understand what it meant then; to us, it was a reaction against communism.

Well, for this party, we rented a hotel ballroom. It was full of young people, and I was one of the security personnel. Our enemies, the communists, found out about this party and decided to pay us a not-so-friendly visit. It ended in bloodshed. For the first time in my life, I saw boys pissing their trousers in sheer terror. It was a violent evening; the ballroom was unrecognizable, and the hotel never allowed us to have such a party again.

At that time, school was true anarchy, too. Nobody knew what they were doing; it was total chaos. I used to go to the girls' school to hang out with my friends during lessons, and the teachers would accept it. My favorite place to hang out was a café called Vava. I spent hours and hours there. I knew everybody; it was a big fraternity. There were many girls, and some of the people there were movie stars, singers, television people, and we would talk, smoke, drink, and have fun.

I was born a boy, from Venus

At the same time, I had a group of friends that were all similar ages, from quite good families. Some of them are still my very good friends today. This group was comprised of very conservative but normal kids. We would discuss politics but were not very active with extreme parties. This was a healthy touch of normalcy for me. We liked to go to the best restaurants, eat great meals, and then go to discotheques.

I also hung around my sister Luisa's friends. They were all medical students and loved to tell very distinct jokes, mostly a very cruel type of humor. Like one of my friends who told a joke in a completely serious tone of voice, about a doctor that had crosses drawn in his stethoscope for the number of patients that died while he was taking care of them. It was a dark time, and it called for dark humor. But they were great people and I loved them.

By this time, I had a best friend. We used to spend quite a lot of time together and talk about everything. He, his girlfriend, and I went out together a lot to dinner or to the movies. These people will remain in my heart forever. (To be frank, I really had a crush on her, but never told her. I am sure she knew about it, too.)

Somehow our lives grew apart. After the Portuguese revolution, I left the country, my best friend went to São Paulo, Brazil, and his girlfriend went with her family to Rio de Janeiro. Much later she came back to Portugal, married another good friend, and had a beautiful and very creative family with him. I still see them from time to time, whenever I go to Portugal.

Amid all the upheaval, life went on. For one thing, I got my official driving license. I had to take a written test, which I passed without issue, and a practical test in the city of Lisbon. I was driving a VW Beetle, and the examiner sat next to me.

"Turn left into this street," the examiner would say, and I would do as he instructed.

At one point he said, "After the light, go right until the end of the road."

I did as he said, but as we entered the road, we saw that two cars were positioned in such a way that there was almost no space to drive between them.

"Mmm. Do you think you can get through?" asked the examiner.

"Sure, no problem," I answered. He looked very apprehensive as I increased the speed of the car. As we approached the cars, the examiner got very nervous. I drove between them, leaving just one or two free inches on each side.

As we passed the cars, he was kind of panicking and told me, "You can drive back, I've seen enough!" And he approved my exam.

My love life was never constant. I had many girlfriends and sexual partners, all female, but I never had one longer than three months. I liked it like this, as I did not have to tell anybody very much about my feelings. I felt very free. Well, the truth was that I was afraid to tell people about my feminine side, and I was not aware of any place where I could find other people like me. I knew they existed, but I had no other information. I had seen other boys wearing girls' clothes, but that was for costume parties.

For me, it was more than that. I had one or two colleagues that were very effeminate. I thought it was because they were gay, but I never felt attracted to men. It was confusing to me, because I had feminine feelings but I was still attracted to women. At that time, I did not know that this was possible. It was something I wouldn't learn until much later. My feelings were totally repressed; I was scared of showing them. I always remembered what my mother told me, that it was wrong to do what I did, as she hit me with her hairbrush.

Politically, my next step was to become one of the founding members of the Christian Social Democratic Youth Party. I was very active in the headquarters and was part of the security of that party as well.

On May 1, 1975, we were defending our headquarters when our communist enemies decided to attack. Again, blood, hardship, and this time even bullets flew all over. I finished the day by escaping with some friends to my family's beach house thirty miles from Lisbon. The night was long and full of alcohol. We were all hungry, and we could not find anything to eat because all the restaurants were closed. Some of us stole some chickens from a local farmer, and we grilled them for dinner at about 2:00 a.m. We paid the farmer for the chickens some days later.

The atmosphere in mid-1970s Portugal was alarming and very disturbing. My studies were not first priority anymore. I was focused on politics, revolution, drinking, nightclubs, and an overall search to become a real extremist. I used to get threatening telephone calls at home, telling that they were going to kill me.

Once again, my mother did not know what to do, so she sent me to London to study English and go to university there.

Personally, I knew I had to leave. I had become a super-macho revolutionary, and like many people in my position, I overdid it. It was just as well that when I left my home country for the UK, I only came back on holidays for the rest of my life.

The Portuguese revolution marked the end of an era. From a country run by a rightwing dictator, Portugal plunged for some years into a communist country before it became a democracy. I know that there is a transgender community in this country, but I have never had much contact with them. Portugal is a very Catholic country, so its LGBT citizens have many challenges, but I can say that with time, they are experiencing more acceptance.

I was born a boy, from Venus

"The soul that sees beauty may sometimes walk
alone."
Johann Wolfgang von Goethe

In London, I finally found normalcy, but I was
incredibly afraid and so used to extremes that I did
not know what it was to be normal anymore. It
was bizarre not to be surrounded by people that
wanted to show aggression and discontent.

But it was a new country, a new life. In the
beginning, I lived with different families as I
learned English. The first house I lived in was
packed with students like me, and I had a
roommate. This was not exactly the place to get
caught in girls' clothes. I had some girlfriends, one
of whom was bisexual. She was from Iran and had

a connection to the Iranian royal family, so one day we were invited to the Iranian embassy for dinner. It was a wonderful day, we were served with a typical Iranian rice dish with saffron and berries. It was really good, and it was eaten with the hands. We were on the top floor of the embassy, a real big room that was made for parties. All people were sitting on the floor, a new experience. Little did I know that some years later, this very building would withstand a siege, one of the first to be filmed live on television. My beautiful Iranian girlfriend would eventually leave me for a woman, which was a new experience for me.

I changed families and finally had a room of my own, which was a good opportunity to start with my girlie things. I bought a car, too, which gave me greater access to the city.

One day, the friends from my old family invited me to go out with the group. There was a beautiful girl named Monika, who had very long blond hair that went all the way down to her hips. That immediately got my attention.

"Hi, where are you from?" I asked Monika

"From Staefa, a small town near Zurich in Switzerland," she answered.

"No way!" I told her. "I know Switzerland very well, I lived there for two years in a boarding school. In Rolle, on the lake of Geneva, and in Gstaad in winter. I love your country."

We had a long conversation, and the next day I invited her out to dinner. It was the beginning of a very special relationship.

We started to go out together every day. I would pick her up from her house, bring her to school, and in the evenings, we would hang around the center of London.

Monika and I decided to carry on studying in London. We both applied to different schools. I went on to finish my A-levels and then attended the engineering school at the City University of London. Monika went to a fashion school, and then to fashion university at St. Martin's School of Art. Later that year, we moved in together and spent five very nice years together in London.

That first year, I went on a road trip for the very first time, traveling from London to Lisbon alone. It was quite an experience, except that somewhere near San Sebastian, the battery of my car broke. I had to replace it, and I had no more money, not even to buy food. I was lucky that there was just enough money for fuel. My parents were waiting for me on the Portuguese/Spanish border, and I finally ate again.

On holiday in Portugal, I spent a lot of time with one of my best girl friends, Margarida. She was the daughter of my old German teacher, and I had known her for a number of years, since we were quite small.

At the end of my holidays, I drove to Switzerland with my father. He then flew back to Lisbon. I picked up Monika, and we drove to London together. There we rented the apartment that became our home.

I had some time to myself when she was in school, sometime I was home. I started to buy female clothes and wear them when I was alone. One day, Monika came into the house earlier than expected. She came in and saw me, I was wearing some white underwear, a very small dress a wig and some hills, it was not exactly tasteful. She opened the door and she stared and me with her moth opened.

"Oh, sorry, I think I am in the wrong house," she said and left the apartment.

I was shaking and full of anxiety, I had been cought.

She then came back, opened the door to see me standing in the same place. "What are you doing with girls' clothes?" she asked.

"I am so sorry, I will take them off immediately, I am so sorry," I said. I ran into the bedroom and removed them. My guilt surfaced again; I was ashamed and hurt. I think at that moment I just wanted to die.

The next morning I put all of my girly clothes in the rubbish bin. It was probably the first instance of a terrible, everlasting cycle in my life. It was always the same. It started by feeling ashamed, guilty, and horrible, then I would swear to myself that I would stop and throw away all of my women's clothing. I would succeed at staying "clean" for several months, but then the feelings would come back and I would buy women's clothes and underwear, until the next cycle would start. Later, instead of throwing them away, I would sell them to a secondhand shop. I have experienced this cycle so many times in my life that I do not recall exactly how many times it has happened.

When we moved into our home, Monika was the cook. The first night she made tomatoes stuffed with a savory rice. It was quite good, but the next day, she did the same rice, this time filled in a pepperoni. On the third night, she changed to zucchini.

By the fourth night, and for the rest of my life, I was cooking. It was something that I became a real expert in. Neither of my wives have been very good at it, but I love to cook. In my first apartment with Monika, I learned how to cook foods from many different cultures: Portuguese, Swiss, French, Italian, Asian, South American, fusion food, and even molecular cooking. It would take some time for me to learn all of this, though. In the first few months, I was not a world-class chef. Well I thank her for the patience, and love.

My weight was increasing, and soon I weighed over 200 pounds. My frustration was increasing as well. I started to explore sex shops to learn more about my feelings, and I learned that there were special shops for cross-dressers with clothes, underwear, makeup, plastic boobs, and all else that was needed. Now I knew where others like me went to buy their clothes. I tried to contact and see them, but this was the 70's. I found out that many of these people were out of reach, either because they were hiding just like me or because they had some kind of timetable that was not compatible with mine. But I started to go to clothing specialists for cross-dressers, even though I always preferred shops for normal women. Well in the seventies there was a crossdresser specialist in London, not too far away from my university in the Angel. The first time I was there I almost fainted, it was like a sweet shop for a sugar addict, there were some ladies, that would help you to find the right clothes, wigs, make up and of course the highest and most exquisite hills. All in a very closed and discrete ambiance. No one would believe that that place was a shop, from the outside.

Many days I would lose myself in women's clothes shops and sex shops between the university and home. There were the first magazines and I was fascinated, if I remember well one was called Tranz.

For the first time, I had a big decision to make. On the one hand, I wanted to become a woman; on the other, I wanted to be Monika's boyfriend. I ended up choosing the second option. It was rewarding to learn about myself, but I was really in love with this girl.

This was also the first time in my life that I was in contact with gay people. This was the 70's and the LGBT community in the UK did not really exist, but London was an acceptance zone for gay people. To see two men kissing on the street or two boys touching each other in the movies was an everyday thing, nothing shocking. One would also see mostly men dressed in shocking clothes. This sometimes meant cross-dressing, but that wasn't all. Some would dress in garbage bags, for example; we called them punks.

At that time, there was also a misunderstanding about transgender people because homosexuality and transgender identity were seen as the same thing. Many people, myself included, thought that a transvestite wore women's clothes to attract men. That was not my feeling. I was not looking for gay men; I always preferred and was attracted to women. I met some people that were near transgender, but they were mostly gay men in Monika's college, so they were out of my boundaries of interest.

As it turned out, at this time I met several people that, like me, came out as transgender many years later, but at the time, we did not know it. One was Monika's best friend, a Scottish guy that transitioned some years ago in London. Unfortunately, I do not have any contact with her.

London opened my eyes to the possibilities transgender people could explore. I found out for the second time that people existed who looked like women but had male penises. There were even people who obtained a vagina through surgery.

I was born a boy, from Venus

That was incredible, my long-life dream. As I mentioned, I had seen this in New Orleans some years earlier, but in London I saw some pictures, and there were even magazines and books that explained the procedure to me.

Monika and I stayed together for fifteen years. She knew about my tendency from a very early stage in our relationship, and she was kind of indifferent to it. That is, I could do it as long as it was not with her. I accepted this and cross-dressed on my own time.

London in the 70's was quite a place. It was the punk generation. The Blitz, the Sex Pistols, and David Bowie were starting to get popular. Monika studied in one of the best fashion universities, and her friends were very special and alternative people. It was at this time that many people groups got emancipated, and the fashion statements were very strong. One of her male colleagues used to wear a striped suit, high heels in sturdy colors like red, and full makeup. He was impressive, and I was kind of jealous. By contrast, my engineering university was extremely conservative.

Apart from mechanical engineering, there were other extracurricular subjects that I really enjoyed.

One was flying. I went to the Cessna flying school to learn how to fly small planes. It was a great experience. I got my pilot's license, but unfortunately, I could not carry on with the annual minimum flying hours so I lost my license in the 80's.

One day, while I was training, I taxied my little Cessna into the field. It was a cold Monday morning, and there was quite a lot of frost. I arrived on the runway.

"XXXXX, permission to take off," I asked the tower, using with my airplane identifier.

"XXXXX, you have permission," the tower confirmed.

I drove to the landing runway, put myself in position and pushed the plane to firewall, meaning to maximum throttle. The plane responded very well and soon we were climbing, that is, until we got to some 200 feet. The motor started to make funny noises and then stopped altogether.

"Okay, what should I do?" I asked the instructor.

He immediately took over the command and started to turn. Since the plane was very low, there was not much of a way that we could land, and in front of us there was a river. Immediately my instructor headed to the golf course just off the runway and landed there. It was bumpy but safe. This was my first airplane incident.

Another area of interest for me was psychology. I took some classes on group therapy, which helped me learn to look at myself with an outside eye.

The last was racing cars. I went to a racing school called Jim Russell Racing School in Snetterton, Norfolk, and was racing Formula Ford cars. It was the feeling of danger that I liked here, and of course I wanted to prove that I was doing manly things. I stopped quite soon after, as I was not born for it.

In summer 1978, I traveled to Brazil on holiday without Monika. After the Portuguese revolution, both my sisters went to live in Brazil, in a town in the northeast called Fortaleza. My oldest sister Ninita and her husband lived there for seven years, while my younger sister Luisa came back to Portugal after several months. I stayed in Fortaleza for quite a long time on that holiday.

Though it was a pleasure trip, I worked as a draftsman in a factory that made all types of cookers, for industrial and residential purposes. The factory belonged to some friends of my family. For many years I had contact with many members of this family. I was really welcome by them and had a very good time with them.

On that trip, I was part of a large group of young people that used to go to one of the family's many farms for long weekends. These were fun times. We would have very large barbecues and drink a lot. I remember one day they gave me a hollowed-out coconut, which is usually for drinking water, except they had filled it with whisky. On one of those weekends, some of the farm workers got married. I was named godfather of the lovely couple and we were dancing the *forro* well into the night after a fantastic barbeque.

At the end of my stay, I made a trip to the largest towns in this fantastic country. I visited the capital, Brazilia; one of the oldest colonial cities, Salvador da Bahia; the largest city in South America, São Paulo; the city of love, Rio de Janeiro; and others.

During my stay in São Paulo, my childhood friend showed me the local specialty, the so-called *"Brasileiras"* — transsexual prostitutes. I had never seen anyone like them before. I wondered at their beauty. Some of them were so incredible, even more beautiful than many cis women. On the other hand, I was shocked with the idea of what they were doing.

I was born a boy, from Venus

Throughout my life, I have traveled to Brazil many times. It is a country where I really feel at home. I often see these transgender women on the road. They are all over the place, but I never looked for them or made contact because I found it really sad that they had to sell themselves to survive. I would really love to help these women to rehabilitate. It is very sad. Many of them are brutally murdered. They disappear without a trace, and the many stories that I know about them are very depressing. Sex work is not restricted to Brazil; here in the United States, in the 70's and even now, similar situations exists. Many are not prostitutes but work for the legal sex film industry.

In Rio de Janeiro, I met with the ex-girlfriend of my childhood best friend. We had a great time with her family, but Rio was more dangerous back then. We did not stop at any red lights at night. Nobody did at the time because people hijacked and robbed the cars that stopped. Once we were on the road, and there was a car chase just in front of us, going at full speed. Then the first car stopped, followed by the one behind it. Two men got out and started shooting at each other with their guns. In Brazil, guns are not allowed, so this was very scary.

My trip from Brazil to the UK was quite difficult. The last night of my trip, I arrived at the hotel very late and very thirsty. I made a huge mistake and drank city water from the tap. The result was that I spent my flight to London mostly in the plane's bathroom, with one of the worst cases of diarrhea I have ever had.

But back to London and normality. Monika and I had a very strong relationship. We had some stable friends, but we were never extremely social people. We used to go to the park and talk about the world, people, politics, and travel.

During the summers, we would spend one month at my parents' house in Portugal and one month in Switzerland, always driving between these countries. We found fantastic places on our journeys, like a great hotel and restaurant called Aux Armes de Champagne in a magical place called L'Epine, in the middle of the fields of the Champagne region of France. It was our overnight point between Zurich and London. L'Epine has one gigantic basilica, a very good restaurant and hotel, a wine cellar, and a dozen houses. I think I took all my girlfriends there over the years.

In 1981, I finished my degree in Mechanical Engineering at the City University of London, and Monika finished her degree in Fashion Design at

St. Martin's School of Art. We still loved each other very much and decided to move to Switzerland to get married.

I was born a boy, from Venus

A New Life in a Known Country

*"Family is the most important thing
in the world."*

Princess Diana

On July 17, 1981, Monika and I had a wonderful day, our wedding in beautiful Switzerland. Monika looked fantastic in a beautiful light crème dress, with a medieval princess cut. I had on striped trousers, a dark grey frock coat, and a beige gilet. I was so thick then that I cannot fit into these clothes anymore. They look like they are for someone twice my size! We first had a Catholic wedding in a small church, then a fantastic day in a boat on Lake Zürich, and finally a buffet dinner in Rapperswil Castle with a fantastic view of the lake.

Many people attended our wedding, including friends and family from Switzerland, Portugal, and England. It was a lovely day. Later in the evening, I phoned the hotel we were supposed to go to for our first night, only to find out that they were double-booked and had no room, so we slept in Monika's very small bed in her childhood bedroom. We then spent our honeymoon in Venice and Rome. There were some issues with the hotels there, too, but we addressed them and enjoyed it a lot.

We then settled in Winterthur, a town near Zurich. Quite soon after, we started our own business, VonGub Creations, designing upscale women's clothing. I was also working with my father-in-law as an engineer in his factory, which manufactured industrial barbecues. This helped us have enough money to live on as VonGub got underway. My wife was the star designer, and I was her business support.

To this day, Monika is a very talented designer and artist. She made the most beautiful drawings and illustrations; now she paints and still does some fashion design. For VonGub, her drawing talents were an incredible asset.

I was born a boy, from Venus

In the beginning, VonGub was a bespoke boutique, and Monika was making dresses to the clients' specific measurements. They were very nice, very expensive, and we developed a good clientele quite fast. We hired a female tailor that worked with us for a long time, and soon we started to make small series of clothes. I would go to Ticino or Zurich to have them made in different sweatshops. We were getting even more customers, and we were enjoying the business. Soon after, we began making collections and selling them through textile salespeople in a fashion house for boutiques. It was clearly 80's type fashion with large shoulder pads, working woman styles, and baggy pants, all made with very nice materials that we purchased from all over Europe. Sometimes we would go to a city called St. Gallen in Switzerland, which is known as the capital of the textile industry, to buy some really fantastic fabrics for Monika's creations.

We held some fashion shows, too. I really enjoyed this. One time we had Miss Switzerland as one of our models, and she was so beautiful. I was the organizer behind the scenes, and had the opportunity to tell the girls what they should wear and to help them dress up and undress. I also helped take photographs of the models to publicize our fashion lines. This was something I really liked as well, and I learned a lot about fashion for my own use by helping the women pose, put on makeup, and wear combinations of garments, shoes, and other accessories.

We were doing quite well. We would go to Paris and Dusseldorf to buy the fabrics at the textile exhibitions, make the sample collections, and then sell them in Switzerland, Germany, and even in the UK through distributors. Financially it was not the greatest profit, but we were becoming well-known and gradually selling our things.

As far as my female side was concerned, you can imagine, it was like a mouse dealing with cheese. I had the chance to try on many of these clothes, make myself beautiful, and be on cloud nine, at least for a short period of time. I loved it. I managed to lose a lot of weight, but some months later, I gained it again.

As I said earlier, I was also working with my father-in-law, designing professional electrical and gas barbecues for restaurants and supermarkets. My father-in-law was a very intelligent person and a great businessman. He had an incredible understanding of people, and he worked very hard all his life. He had a very significant and close friendship with another man who worked for him. The two of them used to drive to the business together. He would have dinner with the family and go on holidays with them as well. I used to go to lunch with them every day and got to know them very well.

It was not such an easy time for me because I was learning German, and as my father-in-law put it, "In our house, we talk the Swiss-German dialect and not the classic German," so I had to learn two languages, German and its Swiss dialect.

My father-in-law's friend Franco was Italian, a great cook, and he came from very old circus families. As a matter of fact, his aunt was married to one of the Knie Brothers, the family that owns the largest circus in Switzerland. It was quite nice; we used to have free tickets and special invitations to go the circus. They owned a zoo in Rapperswil, and we used to go there quite often as well. I still keep contact with Franco that lives in Switzerland, he had his coming out as well, something that I really admired.

My father in law died at a very late age almost one hundred, and I think a lot about him, I have a lot to thank him for. I learned a lot from him: how to work, how to run a business, and how to cook. He was a great cook. He started his professional life as a butcher, he had owned restaurants, and was quite open to trying new foods. I can say he was one of the persons who changed my life. He was not always an easy person to work or be with, but I never had any issues. He always appreciated me and was fair to me.

The first six months in his company, he put me in a special training, so I was working on the shop floor as an electrician, then as a mechanical fitter. After that, I took care of stocks and distribution, and later still I mixed spices in the factory. Finally I started to design equipment, and because of my language skills, I was selling in foreign countries. I designed some of the machines the factory was producing and selling; they were quite successful. I remember that we had a deadline to bring a machine to the market, and for about three months I was working day and night in the factory to design, manufacture, and test the prototype. I was so exhausted afterwards.

It was a great time but very intense. I was working seven days a week: four to five days for my father-in-law and the rest for VonGub. It was very hard, but we were having some success and we loved it. We started to have quite a social life, too, which I loved.

When Monika got pregnant, things changed a lot. We moved to a new apartment on the same street and in the same building as Monika's fashion studio. We shut down the boutique in order to concentrate on selling the fashion collection, which was less time-intensive and more profitable. Until the birth of our son, Monika was actively working.

Just before the birth, Monika was getting a huge, beautiful belly, and she was kind of suffering. Near the expected day, we knew that he was coming late, so Monika started to clean all the windows in our house. The physical exercise worked well, and we had to go to the hospital in Winterthur soon after. It was Monika's first child and she did a fantastic job, and the most fantastic little person I have ever seen, my first son David was born.

The birth went well. As with all my kids, I was present for the birth and gave him his first bath. These are always magical moments I will never forget. I think it actually started to generate some kind of maternal feelings within me. It is so important to support your partner when they have a child. To be there to hold her, kiss her, and support her in that moment, it is magical. When David was born, the first thing we saw was his very dark hair, and as he came out, we realized he had hair all over his body. In fact, all of my kids had this type of body hair at birth that disappeared soon after. The feeling of being the first person to hold my children and put them in the water for their first bath is incredible, something you always have with you.

The first days after mom and son came home were quite emotional, not only because my mother came from Portugal, but also because my wife had a very strong hormonal depression, which is quite normal, but we still needed an expert to come to the house and help us.

Just as she was getting better, my son had a very difficult time with an hernia that was painful and lasted a long time. The poor boy was crying day and night for the first six months of his life. It was very stressful for my wife and I. On the one hand, we did not know what to do; on the other, we were trying to protect him as much as we could.

My wife decided not to work anymore, so I stepped into the company, making the fashion collections and marketing them. There were two great girls working for us — a textile pattern designer and a seamstress — additionally we had some salespeople in different geographical areas. I created a trademark called CreMa, meaning Creation Marques, which was a more commercial fashion than VonGub. This was young fashion made in Portugal at different factories. Obviously, I was not as good as Monica at fashion design, so I would go shopping at boutiques targeted towards young people in order to get some inspiration. Some clothes were even quite sexy, like corsets and mini-skirts with leg warmers. I was designing and giving instructions to the pattern designer the best way I could. We had some nice collections and sales. This was in the early 80's Crema was full of color some colorful patterns, oversized jackets in yellow and orange underneath just a white bandeau and a mini skirt in black or red. Revolutionary fashion for that time, sold mainly in boutiques for young adults.

I was working 24/7, making the collections, discussing and visiting the factories, working with the salespeople, and still working as an engineer with my father-in-law. It was too intense, though, and went from fun to pain.

Once we sold a lot of jean shirts with built-in Swarovski crystals. The people that were supposed to make those shirts could not deliver on time, so I spent an entire weekend with one of my employees attaching the stones to the shirts. Monday morning, I drove to Geneva, some 3h direve, to deliver them. It was hard work. Monika would come almost everyday to say hello and share her ideas with us, but her first priority was David, our son.

The consequences of these excesses came quite soon. I forgot that I existed. I had to recognize that I had limits and could not carry on working full-time as an engineer and doing everything for my fashion house. The result was two collapses within six months. I realized that I had to make a decision. The right one was to change completely, meaning I had to close shop and get a new job.

This meant a new start, new city, same country. It was a great chance that I took and I won.

I started to work for a large international manufacturer of machines for the plastic industry in the Swiss Alps, in a town called Näfels. It was a chance to be with my family and to restart our life. Monika was a full-time mother, and I was only working one job to support all of us. In the beginning, I was just an assistant to a regional sales manager, but my career took a positive turn very quickly, so that I soon became the regional sales manager. It was quite a change. I started to travel; in the beginning mainly to France and England, soon to Spain and India as well. We met quite a lot of friends, and life in the Swiss Alps was very nice indeed.

We lived near a beautiful lake called Walensee, which is surrounded by high mountains. We used to go on trips to this lake and the villages surrounding it very often in summer. Some of these villages are only attainable by boat, with no roads in or out. On top of this lake, there is a village with many ski slopes, and you can ski with a direct view of the lake. In the town of Weesen on the lake, there is a fantastic restaurant called Fischerstube, the source of many pounds of my weight! This fantastic restaurant almost became my canteen, where I met and received my customers.

Our house had a magnificent view of the Glärnisch Mountain. We could observe its changes every single day, and astonishingly enough they were always different depending on the season, the time of the day, and the weather. Since we were in the countryside, I started to take my bicycle to work, which helped me get into better shape.

I was making good money for my family, but I was not completely happy. I had my little cardboard box full of girly things. I used to go to the attic and get dressed there, hiding from everybody, but it was not climate-controlled, so in summer it was too hot and in winter I would freeze. I soon became a workaholic again. I started to travel even more and to work very intensely. This gave me the opportunity to start taking some girly clothes on my trips and dressing up in my hotel rooms.

I was born a boy, from Venus

Hard work was always a good way to escape and not listen to myself. I did it all my life because I didn't want to face what I was. You can fool yourself for a long time, but not forever, and one day it all comes back to you. This, in my experience, is always when you least expect it and when you are at your most vulnerable.

Once I had a long trip, three weeks to Spain and India. I bought quite a lot of presents for David and Monika. When I came back, I gave my son a small Indian toy carved out of sandalwood. It had a very nice scent, and part of the toy moved. He was very sweet and thankful; he obviously liked it.

Later, he asked me, When are you going to travel again? That made me realize that I should probably not bring presents back every time I traveled! I loved my little David, and Monika and I had quite a nice and comfortable marriage, but my traveling was getting very difficult with my family, and we started to discuss this heavily.

Monika got pregnant again, this time in Näfels. I made sure that I was at home for the birth, and my second son, Raphael, came into the world in Glarus Hospital. Raphael had the most straightforward birth. Monika did a great job, I think that being the second time around, she knew how to deal with it better. All went according to plan and on the correct dates. I was holding her and giving support, and when Raphael came out, I gave him his first bath ever. Oh my God, I was, and still am, a proud father of this newcomer and of both my boys. For me kids are so important, the best in the world.

To this point, I would like to clarify something very important to me. As a transgender woman, I remain the father of my kids, because I did not carry them, but I made them. My kids actually still call me Father, but they mostly call me Ella. It is basic biology: I would love to carry and give birth to them, but it was never meant by God. If science could make things so that trans women could get pregnant, I certainly would be on board, even if I think that ethically this could create some problems, that is, from society. Still my kids are the most important beings in my life.

At this time, my business life took another turn. I was very successful, and the management of the company I worked for sent me to France as sales manager of a subsidiary they had acquired some years before. I arrived there, and within the next few days, I found out that the company was in very bad shape.

They were doing all kinds of tricks to stay afloat. They would deliver unfinished machines, invoice those machines that were not working, then sell the invoices to the bank to get fast cash. The issue was that the customers would not pay the invoices until the machines worked. I immediately informed the owners; we had a meeting halfway between both companies, and they made me general manager of the subsidiary company.

This was a real challenge. The mother company could not give me any money because they were having financial difficulties, and the company I was managing was literally bankrupt. I told my bosses that I had to declare bankruptcy. They said I could not and that I should do everything necessary to stay open; otherwise the group would be in serious trouble. At the same time, they told me to sell the company.

These were a very scary six months of my life. It was a real challenge and risk to lead this company. I had to negotiate with the banks, the suppliers, and the customers just to be able to pay the employees' wages. At the same time, I had to make sure that the machines that we delivered were working and that the banks got paid. Sometimes I would pray that the bank would honor the checks that I had signed; it was a very emotional time indeed. Probably one of the most difficult jobs I had to do was to negotiate changes in the payment dates with the suppliers after the products were delivered.

Well, I finally found a buyer for the company, an Italian company in the same market. I managed the full acquisition and transfer of ownership, and in the end, I had to stay another three months to help the new owners as a consultant. It was a hard-working time because we had major negotiations with customers and suppliers, but it eventually came back to normality.

This time in my life had a real impact on my family. I was only at home on weekends, from very late on Fridays to Sunday afternoons. It was too much for my wife who had two children to look after. I could not mend our marriage anymore. My feminine side was getting stronger. I had all my girly clothes in my hotel in France and was wearing them every evening when I was not working. I started to buy clothes from catalogues and have them delivered to my French address.

We then moved to another canton in Switzerland, and I changed my job as well. When I sold the French company, I contacted quite a lot of competitors, and one of them told me, "I am not interested in the company you are selling, but I am interested in you," so I became sales manager there. It was a one and a half-hour commute each way, so I left very early in the morning and came home late at night, and that was when I was not traveling.

Moreover, I was earning my MBA on a part-time basis. I spent many weekends in Zurich, where the City University of Bellevue, located in Washington State, had an international campus. A large part of my studies were done in the air or waiting for planes at the airport, mainly in Manchester, England.

Monika was not happy during this time. We decided to go to a family counselor to prevent the worst, but it was too late. Our marriage had cracked, and we were quarreling all the time.

One day, Monika and I went out of the house to talk with some friends, and then came back home. David had stacked his big Lego blocks in the shape of a coffin, and he was lying inside. He was six years old. We looked at him with great shock. "Stop quarreling all the time, please," he said. We got the message: our marriage was a challenge for our kids.

Monika and I decided to separate, and I went to sleep in the guest room while I searched for an apartment. Alone again, my girly side immediately took over, already in my little room. Soon I found an apartment and moved out. Our divorce came one year later.

Monika was a fantastic mother to these two, she took great care of them. I always kept contact with them and would be a pay and weekend father, did all I could for them.

My First Attempt to Become Myself

*"There is but one cause of human
failure, and that is man's lack of faith
in his true self."*
William James

When I was living alone in my apartment, things changed. I finally had time to be myself. The biggest changes: I lost a lot of weight and went shopping for girls' clothes. I had a great time and started to perfect myself at home.

I was an important manager of a company nearby, working for the owners of the apartment where I lived. Some of my neighbors worked on my team.

I was born a boy, from Venus

One day I was fully made up and dressed up when one of the neighbors knocked on my door. My heart was racing, I did not know what to do. I tried to find out who it was by peering through the curtains, and I managed to see that it was John, one of the engineers on my team. I did not answer and tried to be very quiet, hoping he would go away. He did not; as a matter of fact, we both lived on the ground floor, and he tried to look through the French windows to see if I was at home. I was so scared and felt guilty.

My apartment had almost-direct access to the common building garage. I always wanted to go out as a girl, so one Sunday I decided to dress up and drive around.

I took the car and drove around for an hour. When I came back, I drove into the garage. All was quiet, so I left the car and walked to the door. At exactly the same time another car drove into the garage, but I was already too far away from my car to make a retreat. I just ran and entered my apartment. My heart was beating so fast out of fear and guilt: it was John again.

It was then that I told myself that this would not work. I couldn't wear these clothes and have the professional life I was working for. Again, my clothes landed in the waste bin, but this time I decided to get professional help. I made the decision to be cured and stop this behavior once and for all. I wanted to halt my feelings and my urges to wear women's clothes forever. I would get it out of my life and be "normal"!

To do this, I went to a psychologist. The result was quite different than what I expected, and it changed me for the better. For the first time, I spoke in detail about my feelings, about what I did, my story and behavior to someone else, to a professional counselor. I was very scared, but it was a great step for me to finally open up and talk about my most intimate self.

After some weeks, my therapist asked me, "Why are you ashamed? This is yourself. If you want to be happy, you have to live with it. It is all right to have these feelings and live them out."

My guilty feeling was still very strong, but suddenly I realized she was right. I did not know why I fought myself all my life. Well, I was not completely free yet because I was still very afraid of getting caught.

I soon realized that I was not the only person with these feelings near me, and they were not just sex workers or porn stars. I joined a cross-dressers' club in Zurich, met others like me, and Florence was born. I started to go out as Florence whenever possible; I was not ashamed any more. I lost even more weight; I was quite passable as a woman and was enjoying every single moment of it.

In the beginning, I would leave my house dressed as a man, then go to a public garage or a public toilet that I knew would be mostly empty to change into my girl's outfit. Before I came home, I would do the opposite.

After I grew more comfortable, I would get dressed at home, check to see if the way was clear to go to the car, and then I would drive out as a girl, my heart racing like a horse the entire time. If I was going back, I would change at home, and if I was going to work or to visit some friends, I would remove my makeup and clothes in the woods or in a garage. What a bunch of gender gymnastics!

I met a couple, a transgender woman and a cis woman from St. Gallen. They helped me a lot with my self-confidence, and I started to buy clothes as Florence. The three of us went to bars and restaurants together. These were my first steps as a social girl. I am still very grateful for their support and would love to get back in touch with them. I also started to go to the cinema alone. I was not looking for friendships or sex. I just wanted to live in my girl zone.

I was born a boy, from Venus

When I was dressed up and going out as a girl, I was my real self. I just felt fantastic. I existed in another dimension that I had never experienced before. I was calm, relaxed, and free. The more I went out and met people as a woman, the more I did not want to go back to my daily routine. I started to realize that, as a man, I was functioning but not living.

I had a limited social life then. My time was divided among my work, my children, and my feminine self. Sometimes I would meet with Margarida and my other friends.

I had some love affairs in these early days. Just after my separation from Monika, I started to see a very nice Italian girl who was divorced. We had a nice time together; our sons were similar ages, so we would all go out together.

She was very open. For me, it was early in my period of self-confidence and self-discovery, so I never really told her about being transgender. One day we were alone and did some roleplaying in her house. For the first time, she dressed me as a girl and helped me put on makeup. She then looked at me, and I could see her very surprised face. "Oh my god, you really look like a woman," she said. I am sure she saw me as my real self. She shook her head. "No, this roleplaying is not for me. I don't want you see you ever again as a girl."

Our friendship ended very soon after.

During this period, I started a new and very exhausting job. I was a consultant for one of the best Swiss firms. I was working as a man, but the weekends were for me. I was Florence and later changed my name to Manuela. The reason was that I managed to get a credit card under the name Manuela, since it was very near my own.

I was traveling for my business almost one hundred percent of the time. For a long time, I had my own parking spot in the airport. I was taking a plane every Monday and coming back every Friday. During another period with the same company, I was driving two hours every Monday and two hours every Friday. Any time that I was alone in my hotel room, I was dressed as a girl.

The only time on weekends that I did not wear my girls' clothes was when my sons would come to visit. This happened about every third weekend, sometimes the second one. I would pick them up on Saturday morning, go out to lunch with them, then do some sort of activity. They would spend the night at my house, and on Sunday I would bring them back to their mother. In my apartment, they had their own room, which was a sacred place for them. They had their own furniture and toys in my house. These were some of the most important moments of my life, to have them near me, to care for them. I always cried when I brought them back to their mother, then I would go home, back to my girls' clothes.

I slowly started to come out and told my best friend Margarida and all my new girlfriends. One was an English girl with very big eyes, almost excessively big, and we would go out while I was a girl. She was an artist and a lawyer, a very intelligent person with a huge ego, extremely self-centered. She was a very good painter and performing artist. Though she identified as straight, she had quite a lot of contacts within the lesbian community in Basel. I thought she would be open to me being transgender, so I told her. One weekend we went to Frankfurt, Germany, with me as Manuela. it was the first time that I spent the entire weekend as a girl, day and night. We went to the museum, to restaurants, shopping, and to a club in the evening. I loved it so much that I got depressed when I thought about how I would have to pass as the perfect man when the trip ended. For me, the complete experience was like being myself, and I loved it a lot.

My lawyer friend was not an exact match for me. My kids were always the most important thing in my life, and there was a kind of disconnect between her and them. She was much too self-centered. Just before we separated, she was very depressed; I believe that she finally understood how much my female side meant to me, and for her, it represented a loss. She wanted a man, not a girl.

Margarida helped me a lot in the way I looked and the way I behaved. In the beginning, I tried to be so feminine that it was artificial and not so nice. She told me that, and I started to correct myself with the goal of becoming passable as a woman. Margarida is probably the only person in my life that has seen me as a girl then and now, twenty-five years later. I am so thankful for her support and friendship.

For some months while I was working as a consultant in Italy, I worked with a Swiss man from the canton of Bern. He had a long beard and was quite a highly-respected engineer because he was behind an automatic manufacturing system for a very famous Swiss watch.

Later, when I was working in the Swiss Jura region in a town called Bassecourt, a very tall girl came up to me and asked me if I still knew her. I did not understand at first, but I had met this transgender woman before, as the male engineer in Italy.

We went out for dinner one day, with me as Manuela, and she told me her story. Like me, she had these feelings all her life, got married, and I believe she had children. Then she divorced, and her feelings grew stronger. She went to a psychiatrist, got treated, and decided to become the girl she always was. She gave her resignation from work, and when her boss asked her why, she did not want to tell, but finally she told him it was because she wanted to change her gender. Her boss was the famous CEO of a very large watchmaking company, but he studied medicine and had a fantastic understanding of people. He answered, "That is not a reason to leave. Just take six months, get yourself situated in your new role, and come back to work." This situation was highly unusual for the 90's; her boss must have really been someone with a fantastic vision. I hoped that I would have that same luck one day.

I was alone again, and a voice inside me said that there was a way to happiness, but it would mean a lot of change. My psychologist told me she could not prescribe drugs and would have to send me to the psychiatrist. I was assigned a psychiatric student at the university hospital in Zurich. I saw her once a week for over six months, and I dressed up for every session. I would try to get a meeting early in the morning on Mondays, get dressed and made up at home, go to the appointment, then leave for the airport or my office.

On the way, I would stop in the woods or in a toilet and change over to man mode. I was always so scared that sometimes I could not remove my makeup properly. It caused me a lot of stress.

The goal was for me to start hormones and start living as my true self. I was happy again in my life. I officially changed my name to Manuela and met some new friends. It was very easy because it suited me and felt natural.

Computers have been a fascination for me since they were first released for consumers. I got my first computer early 1980, in the UK, one of the first Video Genies with the Z80 processor. The programs were loaded on cassettes, and we worked with Pascal and basic programs. It was quite fascinating, one of the first computers on the market, but not very productive. I have witnessed throughout the ages the changes in technology with utmost interest and fascination.

With the coming of the Internet, there was a great change to all our lives. We suddenly had access to information that we never had before, not even with books. For the transgender community, the Internet meant we could get informed and communicate with one another, but still be in the closet. The online transgender community, as well as the porn community, grew very quickly.

I started to go online in the early 90's. By the mid-1990s, there were webpages that explained the kinds of medication that transgender people could take to help us transition. Initially I could find information about a pill called Diane 35, but was not able to buy it on the net.

Then I learned more about natural hormones, or *phytomedicine*. By the end of the 90's, I started to buy wild yams and black cohosh after I got some very special recipes. This made me feel good. One day, though, I was showering and touched my breasts, and a tiny amount of yellowish liquid dripped out. I got scared, so I stopped taking those hormones for a few months, only to restart them again.

Before *phytomedicine*, in 1993, my treatment with the university clinic in Zurich was coming to an important step. I was going to meet with the head psychiatrist and hopefully get clinical permission to start my hormones. My emotions started to build up for it; I had already taken some hormones, Diane 35, which I bought under the table. I believe this drug is still used in many countries, but taking such medicine illegally is dangerous, and at that time it was difficult to get. I was anxious for my meeting with the head psychiatrist because I wanted to be cleared for prescription hormones.

Finally, the day came. I wore my nicest dress and makeup and went to the University Hospital in Zurich. The psychiatry student that I had seen for a long time was there with me. This was 1993, another world, and I did not know what to expect.

I walked into his office. It was a cold, white room, and he was sitting at his desk. This looked more like a place of business than my usual psychiatrist's warm, inviting practice.

"This is Fernando Marques, alias Manuela. She is a transsexual." (The word transgender was not in wide use then.) "I have been following her for the last six months, and I believe she is ready and in the need of a hormone replacement therapy," my therapist stated.

"What do you want to achieve?" the head psychiatrist asked me.

"I want to become a woman and have sex reassignment surgery," I answered, "but I have to

I was born a boy, from Venus

live two years as a woman and take hormones before the procedure, right?"

"Yes, that is correct. What do you do in life?" he asked.

"I am a consultant. I work for Mr. H, you probably have heard of him," I answered.

"Yes I have, quite a personality. Do you think that you will keep the same job if you become a girl?" he said.

"I do not know, but I know someone else that works for one of his companies and she kept her job." I then told him the story about the person I met in Bassecourt.

"Are you married? Do you have children?"

"I am divorced and have two sons, nine and five years old," I answered.

I then had to leave the room so that he could talk to my psychiatrist. I waited outside for ten nerve-wracking minutes. In the end, he opened the door and let me in.

"From my point of view, you are just a gay person that dresses up in girls' clothes to get straight men," he said from behind his big desk. "You just want men. For that, you do not need to take hormones or go into hormone replacement

- 125 -

therapy. Anyway, you already look feminine enough."

"What?" At that point I remember feeling like all the blood had left my body, and this was not real any more. How could he say that?

"Well, if you do not agree, come back in six months, and we can discuss it again." He closed the conversation and opened the door for me to leave.

This was probably the worst moment of my life. I wanted to kill myself. Over the next few days, I tried to drown my sorrows in alcohol. I weighed 130 pounds then. I was anorexic and bulimic. To get to that weight, I was vomiting up everything I ate. I wanted to be a nice girl, and hormones mattered a lot to me. I wanted to change, to be myself.

After some days of sorrow, I decided to meet up with other transgender people in Germany. It was quite fun, but my sorrow did not go away. I did not know what to do; I felt hurt and disappointed. I went back to my psychiatrist, who said that there was nothing she could do. I would have to go through talk therapy again and wait another six months for another appointment.

I was born a boy, from Venus

A friend I knew from my time in the fashion industry phoned me just as I was leaving to have my fun in Germany. She asked me if I could help her daughter move. When I came back, it was the day, and I was there.

This was the day I met my wife Karin, helping her friend move. She was eleven years younger than me, a beautiful blonde girl with a very fragile but sporty body. We proved to be quite the team, not just for her move, which went quite smoothly, but also in the following weeks as we got connected.

I invited Karin to go to dinner and a movie with me. I remember we went to see *Cliffhanger*, but honestly I was more interested in looking at and touching Karin then watching the film. After it ended, we went to a French restaurant in Zurich. We spent hours talking until the waiters asked us to leave: the restaurant was closing for the evening.

I enjoyed this young woman's company, and so I wanted everything to be clear between us. Sometime in the middle of dinner, I said, "Karin, I have to tell you that I like to wear women's clothes. I have done this all my life, and it is an important part of me. I have also been seeing a psychiatrist for a long time." I carried on by telling her that I did not want to get caught and hurt again in my life, to feel the guilt I'd experienced again. I think I told her that because of my tendencies, I could understand girls quite well. She accepted this information in a polite but passive way.

I'm not exaggerating when I say that Karin saved my life. I started to concentrate on this great love affair and did not think about my transgender destiny. When she was with me, she cared about me. When she went on holiday in Central America with her sister, I stayed home in my girls' clothes, but when she came back, I played the role of a man and a very good and attentive lover.

It was not long before we decided to move in together. I decided to give this relationship a fresh start and sold or threw all of my girls' clothes away, even my photos and a lot of memories. I still regret this today.

Karin was very nice to both David and Raphael, I must say to the point of replacing their mother when they were with me. Karin was their second mother, and she arranged great excursions for them. Sometimes we would go fishing together, and one time, knowing that David had a tremendous love for bird watching, she organized an outing with a bird watching club near Zurich.

I was born a boy, from Venus

What a day! David knew every bird's species and gender just by looking at them through the binoculars. I was surprised along with all the people in the club that this little guy knew so much. He never gave up his dream to become a biologist, and I am proud to say that he received a prize for the best Ph.D. from the University of Bern the year that I am writing this book.

Raphael is completely different from his brother; he is extremely clever and intelligent, but somehow more minimalist and laidback. He has become an incredible IT person; he has a great understanding of people and situations. They are two very different kids but both brilliant and fantastic.

Apart from a fantastic sexual life together, Karin and I found out very fast that we had quite a lot of common dreams that were open for exploration, like sailing and traveling together. Soon we were taking a sailing course on Lake Zurich, then we got our high sea skipper's license, first completing the theory portion, then the practical exam that started in the Canary Islands in the Atlantic Ocean.

The first time we went out for our sailing lesson, it was a very windy day, so I called up the instructor and said, "It is very windy. Are we still going to sail?"

The answer from the other end was quite pragmatic: "We need wind to sail, you know?" I was laughing at myself and the stupid question I just posed. We had a great sailing day, and what I thought was a strong wind was actually optimal sailing conditions.

Some months after we got together, we moved into a very nice apartment with a sensational view of the lake. In that apartment, I could not keep myself from buying some women's clothes and starting another wardrobe. Karin worked on Saturdays, so that day was reserved for Manuela. I did not go out as a girl anymore, though.

During our time in Switzerland, we had quite a lot of contact with Karin's parents and sister. It was a nice relationship, and they were very nice people.

Quite soon after I met Karin, I decided to change jobs. I was traveling all the time and wanted to stay near home, enjoy Karin, my two sons, and a quieter life. I stepped out as a consultant and started to work for another company in Switzerland. That work did not last more than six months, and an old company I worked for asked me to take over their French subsidiary in Paris.

I was born a boy, from Venus

I liked the idea. It was a fresh start and a new job that would be more stable, with less traveling, even if it was in another country.

I was born a boy, from Venus

A new country, a new life

*"There is only one happiness in this
life, to love and be loved."*
George Sand

I invited Karin to spend a weekend in Paris with me. We had a great time going to fantastic restaurants, meeting nice people, and looking at some of the world's most adored art and historical buildings. Then during this wonderful weekend, I told Karin that I was getting a job in France and that I would love it if she came with me. To my greatest happiness, she said yes, and we started a totally new phase of our partnership.

Until we got settled, I rented a very small apartment on the outskirts of Paris. Karin would come every weekend, and we started to look for a house to start our new life. It was a very intense but unforgettable time. We were high on each other's love.

Soon enough, the time for my trial period at work was over; we were going to stay in France. We found a very old and beautiful house in the north of Paris; as a matter of fact, it was the first house that we visited in that region, and when we revisited four months later, we got it for a very nice price. Karin always had a great eye for houses; all of the houses we've had together have been quite a hit, thanks to her.

One day we went to get our papers from the French consulate. We both presented our papers, and the woman at the counter said, "Mr. Marques, since you have a Portuguese nationality, it is not an issue for you to stay in France because both countries are in the EU. But Karin cannot stay in France. There is only one way she can, and that is that you get married. If she's your wife, Karin can stay in France. In the meantime, we will accept a marriage promise as a temporary paper for her to stay."

Well, we loved each other, so we made the big decision: let's get married. I planned to marry her anyway. We officially got engaged, and in June of the year after we came to France, we were married.

I was born a boy, from Venus

I was traveling for work in France and sometimes in Germany, and at the same time, we renovated our house, a job we both loved. We had quite a lot of work to do; the house was over two hundred years old and the plumbing and electrical wiring especially needed work. Karin is a great painter, so she got to paint most of the house. Meanwhile, I did the woodwork and most other handyman tasks. We decided to have a very creative house, so we bought a beautiful cast-iron bathtub from England and a mosaic from Italy. The house was like us: a multicultural but beautiful place. In the beginning, we had an architect and renovator under contract, but he disappeared with the money we paid him, so we had to carry on ourselves with the help of Fonfon, a local friend, and the son of our neighbor.

The bathtub arrived the day before our marriage. The house was in full preparation for the wedding, but we managed to put the tub in the right place and left it there. It was a very heavy cast-iron piece, so we got eight of our strongest neighbors to carry it up the stairs. The ceiling was a wooden structure, with very strong beams. We were still very scared that it would collapse under the weight of the bathtub. That never happened, thank God.

I was born a boy, from Venus

My second wedding day was June 22, 1996, and I was so nervous that my legs were shaking like trees in the wind. Karin looked like a beautiful princess with a corseted gold and green dress. I was wearing a black suit and a blue bowtie. In the morning we had a civil wedding in the Mairie of Puiseaux-le-Hauberger, then we had a great dinner with our closest friends in the Abbaye de Royaumont. Friends came from Germany, Switzerland, Portugal, France, and Belgium, and Karin's parents came from Slovakia to attend. Unfortunately, nobody came from my family; by this time, my father had been diagnosed with Alzheimer's, and we were all scared to leave him alone in his last days. Nevertheless, it was a great evening with gipsy musicians and great French food and drink in the ruins of this thirteen-century abbey. It is a day that Karin and I will never forget.

All this time, I was hiding in my girl's closet as much as I could. Karin tolerated my female side but was not a big fan of it. I never missed an opportunity to wear my clothes, at home in the morning before everyone was awake, and of course whenever I traveled.

On the evening of September 10, 1997, I brought Karin to the maternity ward of the Isle-Adam

Hospital, north of Paris. Very early the next morning, I drove back and joined her in her room.

Her water had already broken, and she was starting regular contractions. The nurses took us to the delivery room. I was holding my wife's hands while she worked through the contractions and helping her breathe. I felt very close to her in those moments.

Then things started to get quite serious. The baby was already coming out, Karin had no medicine whatsoever, and it was painful. She was breathing very heavily and contracting very well indeed. I could already see the dark hair of our newborn, when all of a sudden Karin cried, "I want to go home! It hurts!"

She was sobbing and started to get out of the contraction rhythm. The doctor told her, 'Come on, Mrs. Marques, soon it will all be over."

But Karin was in pain and started to panic. I had been holding her hands and encouraging her like I was her coach. Suddenly, knowing my wife, I gave her a small slap on the head and said, "Come on, girl, you are almost done!"

I think she never forgave me for the slap, but it worked. She had a few more contractions, and this gorgeous baby just came out, our precious daughter that we called Victoria. She was quite a girl from the first day she came into this world. At the end of her birth, all the nurses came to say hello to Karin, and the doctor was very proud of her. I was so happy for her and so proud to be the father of such a precious, small person. Now I had two boys and a girl, wow what a feeling! As with all my other children, I was the first person in the world to give Victoria a bath.

Victoria grew up in our beautiful, two-hundred-year-old house. She has always had quite a strong character and is a lovely girl, full of energy and life. We tried to make all the necessary things so that our little girl could be comfortable and have fun. Before she was born, I made her a pram out of wood. We also made her a large playhouse and a trunk that she still uses today. Since we lived near one of the most fantastic cities in the world, we would often go to museums, theaters, or fantastic promenades in parks. At the time, Victoria's preferred museum was the Louvre — a girl of exquisite tastes! Later, she started many activities such as horseback riding, at which she excelled.

I came to France to become the general manager of a French subsidiary of a German machine manufacturer. I was hired in Germany by the management that I knew quite well because I had worked for them previously. My first day of work started in Zurich at the airport. I flew to Paris with one of the directors of the German company, Rob. In Paris we rented a car and drove to the site of the subsidiary. We came inside, and the secretary immediately recognized him.

"Hi, Mr. Rob, how are you doing? Were we expecting you?" asked the secretary.

"No, it is a surprise visit," answered Rob. "We want talk to Dave."

The secretary escorted us to Dave's office and opened the door. Dave was sitting behind his desk. He was the current general manager of the company, and he did not know what was going to happen to him. Rob and I entered the room, and Rob and Dave shook hands.

"How are you, Dave? May I present Fernando?" Rob said.

"I am doing great, but as you know, business has been very difficult," Dave said.

"How are your wife and kids?" carried on Rob.

"Quite well. My son is now changing schools, so we are quite busy." As Dave talked, the secretary left the room, and Rob and I sat in two chairs in front of his desk.

I was born a boy, from Venus

"I am glad that things are all right in your private life," said Rob. "Fernando is here with me because he is going to replace you in the French subsidiary."

You can imagine Dave's shock, as he heard these words.

"I knew that you were not very happy with me, but there are rules in France! You cannot do things like this around here. I will call my lawyer," said Dave.

"Sure, that is your right. Fernando will then take care of it. Please spend one or two days with him to make sure that he knows what is going on," said Rob.

We all went out for lunch and discussed the issues that were going on in the company. Rob left soon after, and I stayed with Dave the rest of the day and for the next few days.

I was shocked myself. I had never expected that the company would do things so brutally. Well, for Dave it turned out quite well. We negotiated for some weeks, and he left the company with a very large amount of severance pay.

I got my team together, recruited new salespeople, one from my previous company, and got the finances and service departments up and running. One of the first things I had to do was collect money from clients that had not paid in a long time.

I also inherited some lawsuits, the largest of them with a company in Monaco. I visited the owner there, a very wealthy man with incredible charisma. All went very well, and we started to become good friends.

As I left, he told me, "Don't be disappointed with me, Fernando. This lawsuit will bring me a certain amount of money, and it is just a business." Well, we settled the lawsuit quickly, and he got some money, but not as much as he expected.

Many years later, he offered for me to take care of his subsidiary in Brazil. He phoned me and said, "Fernando, the Prince of Monaco is going to Brazil on October to inaugurate my factory. There is only one small issue. It is now March, and I do not have a factory or anybody there. You have to go immediately to arrange a site for the factory, get people, machinery, and start production by then. Come and see me in Monaco, and we will discuss all the details." I never took that job because the people I worked for would not let me go.

At my new company, the technical center for customers and sales started to grow, and we entered the automotive industry with our equipment.

One of my great friends and supporters in this company was Igor. He was the head of the service engineers, a great person who had a beautiful wife and kids. We had great times together on some very nice business lunches and dinners, working hard but getting results.

I was still traveling mostly in France and Germany. I sometimes took the high-speed train or the plane, and I racked up a lot of frequent flier miles.

One day I had to go to a customer in Brussels and afterwards to the company headquarters near the Swiss border, so I flew from Brussels to Zurich. I was in the business class, which was not very different from economy, except you get some free champagne.

We were halfway to Zurich, the flight attendants were serving snacks and beverages, and all seemed okay.

"What would you like to drink?" an attendant asked me.

I answered, "Champagne, please." She served me, gave me a small bag of nuts, and carried on. I was holding my glass when all of a sudden the plane changed positions, from horizontal to vertical. Yes,

I had to look down to look at my seat neighbor, instead of turning normally on the same level.

My glass of champagne started to go upwards, meaning in the direction of the windows on the other side of the plane. The attendants were flying, hitting the inside walls of the plane, and some of them started to bleed. My immediate reaction was to hold onto my seat as hard as possible. There was no noise in that plane, just people staring at each other with open mouths.

My entire life flashed before my eyes. I realized that I was probably going to die then and there, and holding on to the seat would not make any difference. As suddenly as it had happened, the plane retook its normal position. We felt quite a high level of gravity, and then there was this moment of general relief. I heard a massive chorus of "Ahs" and whispering, followed by clutching of hands.

The captain came on the intercom. "Wow, that was close. I am terrible sorry, but we were affected by the vortex of another plane. Our plane lost stability, and we dropped nine thousand feet in seconds. We have now recovered, and we are climbing to our cruising height." Yes, the incident took a few seconds, but it felt like hours. I have to admit that it took me over six months to recover from this.

I did a great job with the company, bringing it to a profit, but the German owners decided to sell to a very large industrial group that already had representation in France. They offered for me to take over the company, but without the machine sales, so I refused and was out of the job.

This was a new situation for me. I had to reduce all personnel, though I was helping them get new jobs. My coworker Igor started his own service company with another friend. In the end, all my staff offered me and my wife a lovely evening of dinner and entertainment at a major cabaret in Paris. They gave us lots of presents and thanked me for helping them. In my last days with that company, I was working from Igor's office. His secretary handed me a piece of paper and said, "This is for you, Fernando."

It was a fax from my company: a pink slip, which I had already been expecting for a long time.

It did not take long before I found another job, this time as the international coordinator of a mid-sized French company in the metal business, creating industrial storage solutions. Our goal was to expand throughout Europe.

I was born a boy, from Venus

I was working in Paris and Brussels. My family's life changed accordingly; we got a small apartment in Brussels, in Ixelles. Some days we were in France and others in Belgium. Karin would ask me, Where are you this week? I would answer Brussels, so we would travel to Brussels that week; the next week we were in Paris, and so on. We learned to love both cities and both countries.

We had a dog named Sirius, a Labrador-Beauceron mix, also known as a French sheepdog. Sirius traveled with us from one place to the other, and was my partner in crime as far as my femininity was concerned. He would look at me when I was dressed up as if he were asking, "What are you doing, bud?" and then he would give me a hug. I loved that dog. Another member of our family was Merlin, one of the many cats we had; he, too, was an intimate friend of my female version at the time. He stayed with us for a long time, until he passed away. Another cat that followed us for a long time was Semiramis; she followed us to France, Switzerland, and the USA.

Sirius was like a guardian for Victoria. He was so patient with her. From her earliest days in our home, he was with her, and she could do anything to him. I mean, hold and play with the dog's tail, shout in his ear, anything that a small child will do in its innocence. He was a real gentleman. On the other hand, no one could approach Victoria without that dog barking loudly. Sirius was a black dog, and Merlin was a white cat. I have a vivid image of those two sleeping together, the large dog underneath and the smaller cat on top.

With my new job, the traveling picked up quite a lot. In the beginning it was only to France, Belgium, Germany, and England, where I set up different companies, though soon I added Poland to the mix. I spent two years going literally every week to a fantastic town called Lodz. During this time, not only did I have the pleasure of learning about Polish civilization and how wonderful this country is, but I had the time to have my feminine moments in the hotel room, always alone. I bought a lot of nice things for my "wife" who was exactly the same size as me. Well, some things went to Karin, but most went to Manuela.

Traveling became a major issue for me. I didn't get to see my family very much. I had one car in the Warsaw Chopin Airport in Poland, and the other in Airport Charles de Gaulle in Paris. Polish somehow became my seventh language, although I've forgotten a lot of it since then.

Poland was a great place, with beautiful girls, nice people, interesting food, and I may say at that time

I enjoyed the local vodka quite a lot. One week, I was in Krakow, a fantastic city in the south of Poland, which gave me some time to go shopping. Karin was very jealous because she thought I was having an affair with a nice Polish girl. Well, that never happened; I was not interested in having affairs or sex with women or men. I was just interested in being in my room and enjoying my girly clothes and looks; it was like a religious experience for me.

I had a very good relationship with my boss; we used to go to Brussels and Lodz together for the acquisition negotiations of a Polish company. He is one of the people I will always remember fondly. When we were back in Paris, he and I used to go to lunch with our sales manager, who was a very beautiful girl. On our lunches, we would talk a lot about traveling, good food, and different cultures.

After we acquired the factory in Lodz and made a joint venture with a local company, I was there every week as a manager. We bought new equipment and transferred some from France; it was one of my tasks to install the equipment and make the new company work.

It was hard but very rewarding, though the work hours were crazy. Some days we would go to work at 4:00 am and get back to the hotel after the kitchen had already closed for dinner. I had a very nice Polish work companion; we worked and traveled together, and we had great results. One late night, we got back to the hotel and we were starving.

"Hi, we are really hungry," I told the front desk. "Is the restaurant already closed?"

"I will see, sir," said the concierge. He tried to phone the kitchen to no result. "No, sir, it is closed."

"Can we have something in our room?" asked my friend, M.

"I am afraid we do not have a night room service," said the concierge.

M and I looked at each other. Then I looked at the concierge and said, "Okay, we are just too hungry, so we will cook for ourselves."

"No, no, no, you cannot do that!" the concierge protested.

"Just watch us," said M as we walked in the direction of the kitchen.

So we went to the restaurant's kitchen and made our own food. If I remember correctly, we had some scrambled eggs with breakfast sausage. It was good fun. The people in the hotel were not too happy, and they charged us as well.

At that time, people had a very different mentality in Poland compared to the rest of the western world; it was really a communist mentality. I had some trouble adapting and understanding, but still I had quite a lot of fun. Can you imagine a place where most of the people grew up in communist times? They were used to getting all organized; everybody had a specific job, even if there was no work, and then the system collapsed.

On the other hand, a growing number of Polish people were extreme capitalists in a country without capitalist rules. It was quite a shock to see the different mentalities. Our joint venture friends were extreme capitalists; they worked and played very hard but were extremely tough businessmen. Some of the internal laws they had would not even be allowed in the most capitalist western countries.

The work mentality was a challenge in Poland, just after we overtook the joint venture, and the rules were not set. Our workers would come to work very early, wait until they were given something to do, and then do it. When they were finished, instead of telling the foreman they were finished, they just went home. It was the normal way in the time of communism because often there were not enough raw materials so they could not work. Additionally, all of our workers had second jobs. Once, the foreman got hurt with on his second job, so as a result, we could not have him for an entire month. What a waste of time and money.

Another extreme feature at that time in Poland were the roads. They were very dangerous because there were people with new cars, driving at very fast speeds, sometimes over 100 mph, and next to them on the same roads would be some old Skodas or Trabants that would not go above 30 mph. I even saw carts pulled by horses! Old Skodas and Trabants were cars made in communist countries; Trabants were made of plastic and had very small engines. But the most dangerous vehicles were the very long trucks when they were entering or leaving these roads. They were so big that they would block half of the road and the median. Cars had to stop very quickly; otherwise there would be accidents. Every time I traveled between Warsaw and Lodz, I would see a major accident, even if the police were everywhere. Another interesting part of traffic was just outside of Warsaw. Just as the city ended, there was a neighborhood full of prostitutes roaming the streets. They were quite cute, but there were many accidents because all the men were looking at the women and not at the road.

One day a big shock came: the company I was working for was sold, and I had to move on. I was not getting any younger, and I did not want to travel so much anymore. I got a job back home in Switzerland with a very old international company called VR. My new role was to set up a project management team.

I flew a couple of times from Paris to Basel, first for interviews and then to find an apartment for my family and a school for my daughter.

In our last days in Paris, we celebrated my daughter's birthday. It was a day we will never forget. We organized a party with clowns for the kids and champagne for the grownups. My wife went to get the clowns from the train station as I was organizing food and recreation. Karin phoned me, telling to turn on the television; something was happening in New York. I did just that and all the stations in France were broadcasting live as the second plane collided with the Twin Towers. Yes, it was 9/11. The shock was incredible. We could not get away from the television and tried to contact my family and friends in the U.S.

I was born a boy, from Venus

Travel and sailing

"If one does not know to which port one is sailing, no wind is favorable. "

Lucius Annaeus Seneca

I would like to make a short stop here to write about two of my favorite things, travel and sailing.

When I was small, I was quite fascinated by Portuguese colonial history and the discoveries our explorers made. I read quite a lot about sailing and traveling then. I really admired historical figures like Marco Polo; they were my idols.

As you know, I spent time in a boarding school in Switzerland, and at the age of nineteen, after three years back in Portugal, I left my birth country for England and never lived there again.

I was born a boy, from Venus

Adventure and discovering different cultures have always been things I thrive on. When I was living in England, I was fascinated by sailing boats and even thought of building my own. It was a dream that I only partly accomplished. Although I do not have my own sailing boat yet, I certainly have been sailing all over the world.

Traveling was always a constant in my life, probably because I was escaping from myself and did not want to face my truth. I traveled mostly for business and sometimes for pleasure.

How have I put up with a lifetime of travel, you might ask? Easy: I started early.

The first time I flew was at the age of fourteen to go to school in Switzerland. It was the beginning of a very traveled and international life. But extensive traveling really took off when I started to work for companies in international positions.

In the early parts of my life, I traveled mostly within Western Europe, meaning Spain, France, the UK, Switzerland, and Italy. The only exception was the cruise I took across the Atlantic with my sisters. Another country I spent a large amount of time was Brazil, not only during the summer I lived there, but also for most of my business career. I had some of my best experiences there, and it will remain in my heart as one of the countries I like the most. I appreciate the joy of life, comradeship, and great sense of fun the Brazilian people have. On top of all that, I was always in love with their music, the rhythm and joyfulness is overwhelming.

One of the cathedrals of samba in Rio de Janeiro was a place called Oba Oba, which I do not think that is open any more. I remember seeing these incredible gorgeous "mulatas" there. The way these women moved their hips when dancing was magical, and I was so jealous.

Later when I started to work, I would go to Germany, Austria, Ireland, Holland, Hungary, Belgium, and Luxembourg. When I was working for a large Swiss machine company, I started to go out of Europe to countries like India, Russia, the Arab Emirates, Kuwait, and Morocco. Later I started to go to the Nordic countries, Norway, Sweden, Denmark, and Finland, and to Eastern Bloc countries such as East Germany, Poland, the Czech Republic, Slovakia, Ukraine, and many others.

I know all of the European countries, Russia, and many of the old Soviet countries, as well as most of the countries on the American continents, many countries in the Caribbean, and many in Asia.

Some will always stay close to my heart because of friends, culture, food, how many times I visited, or because I had some moving experience there. All the countries that I lived in are in the first line of these countries that shaped me, including Poland. Other countries that moved me deeply include: Germany, India, China, Israel, Mexico, Canada, and Greece. But I also have great memories of other countries all over the world that I know less well. Countries such as Croatia, Seychelles, Argentina, South Africa, Japan, Indonesia, Taiwan, Singapore... Well, let's just say my travels could be the theme for my next book.

But from all my trips, holiday sailing was and still is my preferred way to travel. I have to say, it is one of the reasons that Karin and I developed such a tight bond. As I've mentioned, we learned to sail in a school on Lake Zürich. After we got our sailing licenses, we would charter boats and sail by ourselves.

One day, we had chartered a small sailing boat on Lake Zürich. Karin and I started to sail very well and sailed to the other side of the lake, from Staefa to Wädenswil. As we approached the far shore, the boat stated to slow down. I tried to trim the sails better, meaning I actually started to hold the sails, which made it worse.

"You have to ease the sails, not tighten them," said Karin. I did that, but there was no flattening, and the boat was losing further speed.

"You see, the wind is coming from this side, so we have to tighten them," I said looking at the wind indicator at the top of the mast, which was turning around constantly.

"You know what?" Karin said. "There is no wind. Look at the surface of the water."

We had gone too close to the coast and lost all wind. Somehow, we managed to get back to the center of the lake and found some speed for our return trip. It was a gradual but continuous learning process. Karin and I are now a fantastic sailing team; she specializes in trimming and I in navigation.

Before we left for France, we received our High Seas license from Switzerland. After completing 1,000 miles at sea, we got our certificates and became skippers for both motorboats and sailing vessels. I did many other courses, like solo sailing, radio, and others.

The first big trip we took was a cruise in the Canary Islands with a skipper. We sailed a forty-two-footer called *Kimba*. It was quite a challenge, but we had a great time and met some fantastic friends, one that later became the godfather of our daughter Victoria, a German dentist from a town near Bonn called Ahrweiler. They have remained our friends for many years. There were many highlights on this trip, like seeing whales and some very special types of dolphins. Some days were quite cold, and the wind was mostly very strong. It was our first big cruise on a sailing boat, and we loved it.

We regularly spent winters in the Caribbean, for about seven years. We sailed many of the islands, from Isla Margarita off the coast of Venezuela all the way up to the Virgin Islands. We have fantastic memories of these trips, below are just some of my memories of the places we visited.

During Carnival, which is similar to Mardi Gras, we were in Port of Spain in Trinidad and Tobago. It was one of the best parties in the world, a unique experience. They had fifty-two-foot trucks loaded with loudspeakers that blasted incredibly loud *soca* music. In the back of those trucks were some magnificently sexy dancing girls. Miss Universe was present as well. The Carnival had great competitions for steel bands and costumes. The parade lasted the whole day, from early in the morning to late in the evening. I had never seen anything like it.

I was born a boy, from Venus

The best bar in the Caribbean is the Basil Bar, with its fantastic piña colada, on the island of Mustique in St. Vincent and the Grenadines. This island is owned by some of the richest people in the world, so there are incredible mansions and a really expensive luxury hotel called the Cotton House. The island is well-groomed; it looks like a big, first-class golf course.

One of the busiest bays in St. Vincent and the Grenadines is Canouan. This is because it's home to some of the most beautiful scenery in the Tobago Keys. We were there many times, and every time, the number of boats beside us had increased. The last time we went, there was no place left, so we docked our boat nearby, on an island called Petit Tabac. Well, I must say, our new anchorage was even nicer, with great diving spots to boot.

Canouan is a very large bay, and there are hundreds of sailing boats there all the time, either anchoring for a couple of days or staying there for a long time. In the Caribbean there are not many ports, so many places for the boats are anchorage places. It gives you a really nice pirate feeling, living like a vagabond of the oceans.

On our sailing adventures, we met many families and people that lived on their boats. Some would live on the boats for decades, always sailing from place to place. I must admit that I always thought about this type of life together with my femininity. But clearly one must be aware that there are still many countries in the world where transgender people are not accepted, are even murdered, and some of the Caribbean countries have high levels of homophobia and transphobia.

One incredible thing about sailing in these places is that one always find a Swiss person out of the blue. The Germans are quite everywhere, too, but for a country that has a population of 8 million people, you wonder if all the Swiss are traveling at once.

One day in Belize, we were looking for a small place to anchor between the islands, which are covered in mangroves. As we were sailing southwards, we detected the mast of a sailing ship behind the trees. We found the entry to the small bay, took our sails down, prepared to anchor, and entered the bay at a slow speed.

We immediately saw the other boat, which had two people on board. As we passed the boat, we noticed that they were flying a Swiss flag and that the boat was affiliated with Basel. The two sailors had gone out of sight inside the boat.

I was born a boy, from Venus

We anchored *The Christina*, our boat, not far away. A woman and a man came onto the deck of the other ship, and our skipper shouted at them in Swiss-German: "Do you mind if we stay here?" *The Christina* sailed under the British Channel Islands' flag, so they did not know we were Swiss.

"Of course not! Come on over, let's have a beer together," they shouted back.

We took the dingy to their boat, where we shared some beers and had a long conversation. "I am Rob, and this is Ellen," the sailor said as we boarded. "We decided to take some years off work, bought a sailing boat in France, and have been sailing now for one year. We crossed the Atlantic, spent some time in the Windward Islands, and now we are on our way to Panama and then the Galapagos, but we have time and want to have fun." We had a nice evening with them, but we all went our own ways.

On the same trip, we were in one of my favorite places ever, an island called Rendezvous Caye in Belize. The island has a coral reef on one side and a deep underwater wall on the other. Karin and I are still debating the exact number of palm trees. I believe it was fourteen, and the only inhabitants of this secluded island were the pelicans.

I think of it as the dream of a lonely island in the middle of the ocean, the dream of *Robinson Crusoe*, which takes place in the same region, though further south in Trinidad.

We were returning from Rendezvous Caye when we saw a small island with some small houses and some kind of fishing boats docked in front of it. We anchored nearby and took the dingy to see what was going on there.

All of a sudden, we saw a older man coming out of a house. He called to us, "What do you want here?" He did not seem amused.

We approached him in the boat and said, "Hi, do you have any fish to sell?"

"No, we do not sell fish here. We are a restaurant."

We looked at each other, very puzzled. The house certainly did not look like a restaurant, and in the middle of the mangrove islands, where would they get their customers?

"Okay," our skipper said, "please reserve a table for tonight for five people."

The answer was, "Wait, I will see if we have any places left." The old man entered one of the houses and about ten minutes later came out and said, "You are lucky, you have the last table. Dinner is at

6:00 p.m. Please do not be late. There is only one set menu, chicken."

We were really surprised by this place, but since we didn't catch any fish and didn't have much to eat, it was the only alternative. We arrived punctually at the restaurant, that we had by then dubbed "Restaurant at the End of the World." To our astonishment, the bay in front of the restaurant was completely full of boats that were not there before. As we entered the small restaurant we were astounded. There were some fifteen tables, all completely full. We sat down and were served quickly.

The old man came to our table and asked, "Where are you from?"

Our skipper answered, "From Switzerland."

Then the old man said, "I do not like Germans. I am Dutch and left Europe during the War. I hate Germans." He was not very friendly, so we did not tell him that two of the people at our table were from Bavaria.

The old man started to tell fisherman tales, like, "Be careful around here. There are Mantas so big that they will eat people." Or, "I saw a manta that was bigger than a white shark." It was a very interesting and entertaining evening. We found out that this place was well-loved by the so-called "native tourists" in the area.

Some of my favorite sailing trips have been with friends of our little family. When we lived in Switzerland, our daughter Victoria had a very good friend Celine, a nice half-Swedish, half-Belgian girl who went to school with her. It did not take long for Karin and Celine's mother Olena to start a friendship. They had some things in common because they could both speak French, and both Victoria and Celine were the same age, about seven, and only children.

One day they came over for dinner with her father, Eric; I was cooking as usual. As with everyone we invited to our home, we told them about our sailing adventures and showed them some photos. They were visibly excited and interested in what we told them. It was a great evening.

A few days later, Eric phoned me and said, "We really enjoyed dinner with you. Why don't you come to our house on Saturday? Will you be around?"

I said, "Thanks for the invitation. I am okay with Saturday, but let me ask Karin if it is okay for her as well." I continued, "By the way, we would love to go sailing with you guys sometime. What about renting a boat together for the holidays?"

Eric said, "Sure, why not? It could be fun."

The result of our conversation was a gorgeous holiday in the Seychelles on a 38-foot Moorings catamaran called *Serenity*. After a stop in Vienna, we flew to the international airport on the island of Mahé. We took a taxi and went down to the Providence Marina to get our boat.

For the first two days, we had a skipper to help us understand the boat, and for the remaining two weeks, I was the skipper of a two-family crew. The boat was quite large for all of us, so Eric and Olena had one cabin, Karin and I had another, and the two girls had their own.

Already on the first day, as we set sails to go to the north island, we could see how Eric was getting bitten by the sailing virus. We had a great time on this trip. The winds were phenomenal, the area one of the most beautiful I know, the company so good that we are still friends now, and they know about Ella.

On this trip, I had some fishing incidents north of Praslin Island in the Chevalier Bay that I will never forget. I was getting frustrated with my fishing prospects. Nothing was biting, even if I had bought the best local gear.

One evening, we went to the local restaurant, and I drank a little more than usual. I remember leaving the restaurant and going to the beach. It was already night, and we were illuminated by the moon. It was so nice. As we walked toward our dingy, we could see thousands of small white crabs walking on the beach. We took the dingy to our boat and had the wonderful idea to go fishing right then. I got my fishing gear, cast the line into the water, and started to bob up and down to try to catch something.

It was not more than five minutes before I noticed something bite the line. "We have fish!" I screamed and all came to see what was going on. As we reeled the fish into the boat, we discovered a large, young barracuda. It was enough for six people to eat.

My second incredible catch happened when I was bathing in the same bay next to the beach, and I saw a gray snapper swimming next to me. The fish was between the beach and me. I decided to try to scare him onto the beach, and it worked! The fish swam very fast in the wrong direction and got stranded. I came up fast behind and picked him up out of the water. It was a nice snapper to eat.

I was born a boy, from Venus

We continued to have a lot of contact with our friends, and met with them regularly. One day, Eric asked me, "What about this year? Where are we going to sail?"

We then found a gorgeous destination, Croatia. We sailed on a 45-foot Beneteau called *Makci Lou II*, again for two fabulous weeks. We started in a town with a remarkable history, Dubrovnik. I was astonished to see how well it was rebuilt after it was destroyed some years before in 1992 during the Siege.

In some places that we sailed or stopped, we still saw reminders of the war. This area of the world has such a wonderful history that is visible everywhere, including Spilt, a very old medieval town, and Korcula, where Marco Polo is supposed to have been born.

One evening, we anchored our boat in a bay off the coast of Mljet, where our daughters soon found a lot of friends. They had played during the day and wanted to have dinner together. So, after talking to their parents, we all went to the same restaurant and made a kids' table with about twelve kids! They all came from different countries and spoke different languages but were communicating and had a great time together. In the end the kids made a show to the parents, each one presenting something from their own country.

In August, the Dalmatian coast is very busy, full of tourists, so it was not easy to find places in the ports if you don't arrive very early in the day. We used to say, "The Italian fleet is coming!"

One year later, we took another trip together, but this time with two boats in Greece. We started on the island of Kos. It was late in the season, and the weather was getting very rough with strong winds. One day Karin, Victoria, and I docked off the Isle of Simi, where we spent some time bathing in a gorgeous bay, then we left for Rhodes.

Unfortunately there was bad weather. We could see thunder and strong wind coming up against us. We arrived quite late, and some very difficult waves made us run very close to the beach as we entered the port. We were so scared that we entered at full speed. All went well, though. We were very respectful about bad weather and the sea, and we had a great time.

Eric and Olena became very professional sailors. Some years later, Eric bought a lovely, brand-new aluminum boat in the north of France and sailed it to Sweden. I was, and still am, slightly envious.

I was born a boy, from Venus

The last time that we sailed with Eric was in this boat, in Norway and north of the Artic Circle.

We certainly love to sail. We sailed in many more areas, such as Brazil, the south of Spain, Portugal, and different areas in Greece. I hope to start sailing in North America, especially on the Pacific, the only ocean that I haven't yet sailed.

Somehow when I was sailing, my femininity was not there, but all women have their dressed-up and their dressed-down days. That is, I did not have my girls' clothes, but I was always myself. I still dream of going sailing as Ella, in a bikini.

Back to the Alps

"I turned into a workaholic to the point of where my health was in jeopardy.
Tab Hunter

Well, probably not exactly on top of the Alps, but surely back to Switzerland, in Basel.

Basel is a very nice town, bordering both France and Germany. There is even a point where all three countries meet. We rented an apartment in a neighborhood there called Gundeli. It was not necessarily the best part of town, but it was very convenient for my new job at VR. Karin was not so pleased because it wasn't close to the French kindergarten where Victoria was attending school, but it was only a provisory place; even the furniture that we brought from France was in a depot.

As I returned to Switzerland, I started to explore my womanhood again, and I joined a transgender club in Basel. I was going out again as a girl.

One evening I was going out with some of the girls, and Karin said, "Let me help you with your makeup".

"That is so nice of you, thank you," I said. We were in the bathroom, so she came toward me and started to apply some pink eye shadow.

"I think this color will be nice for you," she said, brushing the powder over my lids. "Where exactly are you going tonight?"

"We are going to have dinner in the restaurant of a hotel in Solothurn, then we will have some drinks there at the bar," I said. "I don't know many of the people, just a girl from Basel called Miranda."

"That looks good," Karin said as she finished the shadow and started to apply an eyeliner. "Don't move, otherwise it will look bad." She carried on. "You have to tell me what type of people are at these meetings and what you talk about."

"Sure," I said, trying not to move as she waved on mascara. "You know, they are very normal people.

I know some are from Bern, and they work for the government; others are business people. Most of them are married. We talk a lot about our wives and our hobbies."

"Some lipstick, and you are done," she said as she applied a pinkish color to my lips.

"Mmm." I tried to talk, but nothing much came out.

"There you are." She leaned back to study her work. "You look very pretty," she said.

Karin is a great woman and a great companion. We make a great team, and we love each other very much. Towards Ella, Karin has her ups and downs, but she has always given me a lot of support. She gave me quite a lot of beauty tips, advice about what to wear and what not to wear. But one must take into account that this does not come naturally for her; she does it because she loves me.

For a woman who is not lesbian, to tell her partner how to be beautiful, something that is usually a prerogative of femininity, can be very tough. If it is just a simple roleplaying game, it is quite acceptable, but when things get more serious, and the obvious changes due to hormones or even surgery take place, it is a complete different game. Much later, when I started my transition, Karin told me, "My husband has to die. Then I can probably accept Ella."

One day, I left the apartment as Ella to wait for the lift, and as I was coming out, my neighbor was on the first floor. I left the lift without saying anything. He just looked at me, and I just carried on. My heart was beating at such high speeds that I thought I was going to have a heart attack.

He clearly saw me, and I thought he recognized me, but looking back, I think it was my fears playing tricks on me.

I was going out regularly with the girls in Basel. The club's meetings were once a month, and I went to every one for a nice period of time. It was a lot of fun, and a great excuse to go out as a girl.

That is, until one day I got a reflux outbreak while I was drinking a pink cocktail. I took it as a sign to stop my transgender actions. This was a big mistake. In reality, the reflux outbreak was just a sign that I was getting fatter and not eating healthy. I am sure now that my guilt just came on in a big way, but nevertheless, I stopped. As usual, I started my cycle of throwing away my girly clothes, buying new ones later, and regretting the whole thing.

I was born a boy, from Venus

I was working a lot in my new job. I liked it, was doing great things, and was well-respected. I was going through a period of meeting many people, many of whom are still my friends today. Most of them do not know about my transformation, so I am very interested to see what their reactions will be when they find out. In the beginning, I was not traveling much. I had time for myself, my family, and my hobbies. With time, though, I started to go to the U.S., then to Brazil, and increased my travel miles quite considerably. Karin was a great mother and homemaker; she had the family under control.

This allowed me to become a real workaholic again. It gave me the opportunity to concentrate on other things than myself and my feelings. Looking back, work was always a way to escape my feelings; it was like another type of addiction. I had no time for me; family and work were all I had time for. But usually workaholic came together with an increase in alcohol consumption, often with cigarettes and a complete increase in all types of addictions, like online poker.

My smoking was getting bad, with over two packs a day at its worst. One day I decided to quit smoking. I did for about two years and gained twenty-five pounds. My weight was always an issue. When I was alone between my marriages, I lost a lot of weight, getting as low as 130 pounds. When I was with Karin, my weight grew more or less to a normal 165 pounds. Though much later I got back up to 200 pounds, I lost it again and have returned to normal.

I think my weight has always been a struggle because good food has always been important to me, from the time my mother force fed me to make sure I grew to be a strong boy. As a result, my food habits were somehow the biggest enemies for me to lose weight. When I started to cook for myself, I tried to reproduce the food from home, but I soon started to look for more international recipes. I enjoyed food from all over Europe and China. With time, I was cooking many types of cuisine.

At the same time, I was going to some of the best restaurants in the world, which were a great learning experience. I mean some were even Michelin-starred: from Bocuse in Lyon, Tour D'Argent in Paris, Tavares in Lisbon, Kronenhalle in Zurich, and so many great places in London, Munich, Frankfurt, and Milan. I can say that every single bit of fat in my body was either made by a great cook or by myself.

Basel, I found, is an excellent place for food. For one thing, it has the largest concentration of

Michelin-starred restaurants in the world, and for another, you have Alsace as neighbor, an insanely good place for wine and food. Most wine regions in the world are also good food regions. The only exceptions are Brazil, where the wine is not that impressive but the food is fantastic, and most Asian countries, where wine is not really a great focus. In North America beer partly replaces wine culture, though the wines here are impressive as well.

Looking at all of the cuisines in the world, some I believe are more incredible than others. The list is very large, but I must say that Japanese, Chinese, French, Mexican, and Brazilian food are some of the best. Once we moved to the U.S., I found that American food can be very good to exceptional; it is a melting pot of international cuisines and, except for fast food, it is very good. I prefer a good quality hamburger over Italian American cuisine, although there are some first-class Italian restaurants in the U.S.

Within the last few years, I have changed my diet. I am now focusing on more healthy and sustainable food. I've almost entirely given up meat, and I am mostly pescetarian, meaning I eat fish, milk products, and mostly vegetables, grains, and fruits. I cook accordingly, and I must say that it can be very tasty. I have learned that you are what you eat, and your health has a lot to gain or lose from your food choices. Being transgender, there are several medicines that I take, and good food supports them, while bad food does not. The results are quite visible in the blood tests that I regularly do: no more cholesterol, low sugar levels, and very low blood pressure.

I like sushi a lot. Indian vegetarian food is very tasty, but I also enjoy Italian cuisine with its strong garlicky flavors. You may be surprised to learn that Mexican food does not have to have meat; as a matter of fact, there are many famous vegetarian dishes from this country. A good vegetarian Cajun ragout can be special, and now with vegan burgers or even soy chili, one can have great foods that are healthy as well. Vegetarian, vegan, pescetarian, or omnivore is in any case a personal choice, and I believe one should listen to one's own body to understand what they need. People are so different; the healthiest things for one person can be poison for others.

I must add here that I train at the gym about three times a week. It is so important to keep healthy, mainly when you are going through HRT and your entire body is changing. I regularly track my resting heart rate to make sure it does not shoot up like a rocket, though the tendency is clearly there. We have Ariel, a family trainer who comes regularly to help me and my wife keep in shape. She is great, in all respects. We feel so much happier and healthier with this training; it has been a big game-changer.

Returning to our Swiss period, Karin and I settled in and bought a new house in Reinach near Basel. We had a great time from the design of the house to the interior decorating, so that it was quite different from all the other houses around us. It was a really luxurious place with a spacious feeling throughout. We decided to enhance this by taking away many walls within the house. It gave our home a fantastic feeling of space and warmth. Quite soon it became an important place for the growth of my daughter, Victoria.

At VR, the CEOs were constantly changing. Most of them stayed only for two to four years. One of them was a very good manager; he had risen to a high rank in the Swiss Army, and he was difficult but fair to deal with.

The entire company was afraid of him, but I could see he was very good with people. He was a good listener and decision maker. His team was not big but very effective. The results were great. When he came, the company was near bankruptcy, but he turned it around, making a profitable, growing company. It was probably the best and most profitable time I had at VR.

This person was a great balloon pilot. My team at work once gave me a birthday present: a ballooning trip with my boss. What a fantastic day! Karin and I got up very early and drove to Flims, a very nice town in the Swiss Alps. There were a group of balloons going out that morning, at 6:00 a.m. I found my boss quickly, and we started talking.

"That was an early wake-up call for you if you came all the way from Basel," he said.

"Yes, but we are so excited about ballooning with you, we could not sleep the whole night," I said, "and we are happy to be on time. May I present my wife, Karin?"

"Hi Karin, nice to meet you. Is this your first time in a balloon?" he asked.

"Yes, I am afraid so," she replied. "Which one is yours?"

"The one down there in the back," he said, pointing to a balloon that was laying on the ground. Karin and I said nothing, but looked at each other. My boss continued. "But first things first, you have to sign the disclaimer, and I have to ask you if you intend to commit suicide before you enter the balloon."

"Okay, not to my knowledge," said Karin, and I said with a hint of humor, "Not now, doing okay."

We had to sign some paperwork, then he and his crew started putting hot air into the balloon, so that it lifted quite fast into the vertical position. After a short photo on land we entered the basket.

My boss activated the burner, and we started to gently lift into the air. It was a small basket, probably meant for no more than four people. As we climbed, our view of the Swiss Alps grew from fabulous to magical.

"Wow, so fantastic!" I said. "It looks like I am an angel in the clouds. Karin, look down."

Karin answered as we were approaching some 2,000 feet above ground, "I don't feel so great. It is fantastic, but I'm *not* used to these heights. By the way, is there a safety belt?"

My boss and I laughed at her comment. Despite this, it was a wonderful day. Karin was a great sport; she was slightly scared, but she took it like a real lady.

After this CEO, there was a group of shareholders that bought many of the shares when our company was in a bad shape. The shares were then around 80 cents of a Swiss franc. Well, later these investors sold their shares for over 12 Swiss francs, making many millions for themselves within just about four years.

Another one of the shareholders, a German nobleman, decided to become majority shareholder of this company. He bought most of the shares and placed a new CEO and president of the board at the top. Our costs exploded. The new CEO employed a lot of his old work friends from the previous company; he changed the organization, and soon the company was losing money.

Since that CEO, the main shareholders always managed to get CEOs that did not come from the business and did not have much knowledge of what they were doing. I believe it is the new trend in many companies: CEOs work for their own money and not to develop or add value to the corporations they lead. The times where the owner was the CEO have gone, which is unfortunate because those people made mostly good and fast decisions that often were positive for society. Now there are many professional CEOs; some of whom have wages in the millions, working for companies that have very large losses. Happily, there are still very good ones that develop value for their companies, develop the people they work with, and the communities where they are.

In the last decade, the general market growth in the western world has been lousy, and many companies are thus in poor financial situations. Adding to this, many companies do not employ older people with extensive experience in order to reduce costs, so after a certain age, it is getting difficult to get a job, even if you have a fantastic CV. It is scary because sometimes, it feels as though there is no reward any more for achievement in the business world.

I began a new job as strategic marketing manager in the company's headquarters. This meant there was not much international travel but a lot of work, and I sometimes worked very late in the office. Once I even had a telephone conference with the U.S. that started at midnight! It was a rough time. My commute was an hour and a half each way, and I did not have much time for myself, or even for my family.

One day, one of the management team asked me if I could get a quote for an exhibition booth from a company he knew. I did and listed them as one of the candidates for our largest exhibition in Berlin. The same evening, while I was driving home at

10:00 p.m., I got a phone call from my boss, the marketing manager of the group.

"Hi Fernando, you have good reception?" asked A.

"Sure, A, I do. I am driving home to Basel, but how can I help you at this hour?" I asked.

"The boss wants to talk to you, just hold the line," A said and patched our boss through.

"Hello, Mr. Marques, I understand that you were correct with the information you sent to Sven, but you exceeded your competencies, and I am firing you on the spot, here and now. Do you understand?" said our boss.

"Well, I," I started to say and was brutally interrupted by him.

"I will not accept any opposition. Just shut up and goodbye." He hung up.

A was still on the line. "Sorry, Fernando. Sven was complaining, and he was not very pleased."

I answered in good German, "You can all go to hell." Well those were not the exact words.

The answer from A was "Let's talk tomorrow on the phone. Drive safe."

The next day I got a phone call, inviting me to a meeting with the same big boss in Munich. During this meeting, I got my job back, only I was not a marketing manager anymore, but a key account manager.

"Mr Marques, taking into account your experience, know how and all that you have done to VR, I decided to keep you, only I want you to go to work in the sales department and leave Marketing." Told me the big boss, that is why I had to get up so early, take a flight to Munich and after the meeting come back to Basel. I have to say they found my replacement very fast, within days.

This was another life entirely. I was traveling again and in a big way. I spent more time in the air than at home. One year I flew over 350,000 miles! It was very good for the business, sales with my customers exploded, but I almost exploded along with it. One thing was clear: I had gained weight, and my health was not doing well.

I had years where I made a multitude of round-the-globe trips. They were interesting because I had to pick three cities to stay in, and the trip had to be a minimum of ten days. I traveled most of the time in economy class. I also had to make crazy, excessive trips, like flying from São Paulo to Zürich, having a one-hour layover, then flying from Zürich to Shanghai, with a total flight time of twenty-four hours.

I was born a boy, from Venus

Some of these trips were quite incredible. In 2010, there was an active volcano in Iceland with a very difficult name. The result was that European air traffic control was shut down and traveling became a nightmare. Saturday of that week, I woke up in São Paulo and was going to fly back to Zürich to go home. My travel agency phoned me in the morning to see what I was going to do.

Well, this led to another small adventure. I took a flight to Fortaleza, then to Lisbon, arriving early on Sunday morning. At that time the flights to Lisbon were still open; I think I got the last TAP seat. Then I tried to go from Lisbon to Switzerland where my family was. The alternatives were to take the train – three days later because I was not the only one with this idea – or take a taxi, which would cost me a fortune. I decided to stay put and wait until the air traffic control would be open again.

The only two things I could enjoy on many of my trips was the good food and my hotel room escapades that became a daily thing. Sometimes I would stay in Shanghai, São Paulo, or Bangalore for the weekend, so I would go sightseeing or shopping. Having short-time sex never interested me, and I found prostitution disgusting. It was never my thing. I did like to go to live music clubs and other places frequented by beautiful, classy women. I loved to see how they dressed and moved. I was fascinated by all that is feminine. Feeling like a woman always meant to me that women must be respected, and I have always fought for women's rights.

I was quite successful as a key account manager, appreciated by my peers and my customers, and I was doing very well. I managed to bring big business and good deals to VR. On the private side, my family suffered, as I was not at home very much. Sometimes I was away for two weeks, then came home one weekend just to leave again.

My wife was great and understanding. She was a fantastic mother who took great care of her little love, but at this time my daughter was making some very alternative friends, almost criminal, that were not exactly what we thought was good for her. Some of these people were offering her alcohol, smoking, and drugs. We started to have an increasing number of conflicts at home

One day, one of my peers called and asked me if I wanted to join his company in the U.S. I am not giving his name here because I am not sure how much he would approve of it, but he was someone who always mattered to me. In the beginning, when he came to VR, he was not very well-liked, but I had quite an admiration for him. Later I got to know him better, and he proved to be a good person, supportive, and correct. During the many years we were together, sometimes he made comments that led me to suspect he knew about my femininity. One day, we had a team building event for VR employees, river rafting in Colorado. It a lot of fun. As we were waiting to be picked up by the bu,s he saw me without my top and told me, "Wow, you have big tits." This was three years before I started HRT.

I asked Karin if she wanted to come with me to America, and she immediately said yes. Actually, her words were, "My bags are already packed, let's go!" We were also persuaded that it was time to get Victoria some fresh air.

During a phone call, I asked my peer, "Where do you want me to live? America is very big, and I believe I will travel quite a lot."

"That is up to you. Anywhere on the American continents, from Canada to Argentina." He said, "I do not live near the headquarters either."

"Okay, what about the Bahamas?" I asked him.

"Come on, man, that is no good for flights," he said.

"Okay, let's try South Florida, around Palm Beach," I told him. "My wife knows the area, and I have good friends not far away. Besides, there are three airports."

"That is okay with me," he said. And that was that.

Time to Change Continents

"I was definitely living fast. I was working, traveling a lot, playing. I didn't stop. It all became unbalanced".

Kate Moss

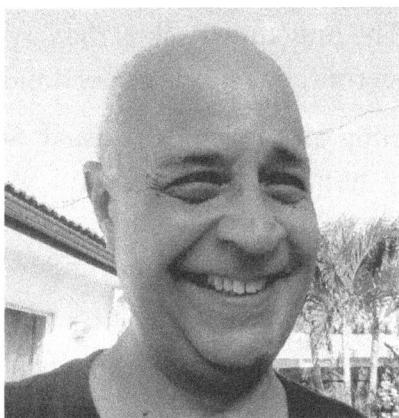

The first thing we looked for in the U.S. was a school for Victoria. It had to be international, in a place where she had choices for her future. In the beginning, we looked in Palm Beach, and in nearby Boca Raton, we found a school with an International Baccalaureate program, where Victoria could start just after summer holidays.

Karin, Victoria, and I came to visit the school, and we were quite impressed. Somehow it reminded me of my days at Le Rosey.

I was born a boy, from Venus

I negotiated my contract as well as I could, and we moved to Florida. The first three months we lived in a hotel. During this time Karin looked for a home while I traveled for work. We bought a house not far away from the beach in Boca. This is probably one of the most fantastic places I know in the world. It is well taken care of, and even if it is a very new town, it is well-organized and quite beautiful. The only drawback is the city paperwork to get any permit, but this is understandable.

I was traveling all the time, as usual. Sometimes I would stay home for a week and work, in the beginning from the hotel and later from home. Karin was again a great home finder and family coordinator.

Victoria had a real crisis, though. She had a multitude of friends in Switzerland that she had to say goodbye to. As a matter of fact, she had a huge goodbye party, and we hosted over one hundred people.

In the U.S., she had to start all over again. She did not know anybody in the beginning, and it was not only a new country, but a new language for her.

She was lost for a time, but from the first days she came to the U.S., she went to school and started to meet people. Soon she had a boyfriend, and life changed for her. Then she went through a period of a successful, gradual adaptation. Her English language skills improved dramatically. She became completely integrated, while keeping many of her European contacts, friends, and communication skills. She turned out to be a great student and later entered college in Tampa. She has quite a character; some years ago she started dating a really fine American boy, and they are still together. They are quite a good match.

One of our first visitors in Florida was my second son, Raphael. David followed sometime later with Gaby, his long-time girlfriend and now wife. During all these years, though our family lived in different places, we have always been very close and loving. Those three kids of mine are my biggest and deepest love; they matter more than anything and have always been a source of inspiration.

Soon our storage containers arrived from Switzerland. We moved to our new house, and our lives settled down. I had more freedom to do what I always did behind closed doors. My habits carried on, traveling and being the girl I always was in the room and the man outside.

Karin started socializing quite a lot locally. Soon she was volunteering and making some great friends. One of the most wonderful things that we have in Florida is not only a fantastic infrastructure but fantastic nature. On one side we have the Everglades, a real wildlife park with such a diversity in flora and fauna. We live next to the Atlantic Ocean in Boca Raton, with coral reefs not far away, populated with creatures like turtles, sharks, rays, and an incredible variety of fish. My wife's volunteer work concerns a great institution called Gumbo Limbo that takes care of sea turtles. Karin has done a fantastic job there. She became a member of the board of directors and is quite active, chairing some committees. Nature was always a theme for us; being sailors, we love the outdoors and hate pollution and other manmade disasters.

Under the leadership of the person that brought me to the U.S., VR Americas grew profitable. We were doing intense work on two sides, both strategic growth in a depressed market and cost-reduction actions. I was very happy and proud to be on his team. On top of everything else, I was giving technical support and training to our sales force and customers.

During my professional career, I met as many great managers as I met lousy ones. Unfortunately, with the years, many very high level managers got more worried about their income and pleasures than the wellbeing of the company they were working for. One of the great managers of VR was W, the last CEO before the baron took over this company.

The person that brought me to the USA is on my list of incredible people. My God, he was not always easy to deal with, but a positive, supportive, and very interesting person. We had the most incredible meetings and negotiations all over the world like in Shanghai, Tel Aviv, northern Germany, all over the U.S., and Brazil. He is a tough negotiator, and he never forgives. When someone crosses him, there is no way back. We still have regular contact, though I own my own business; I hope he will be my customer now.

One day I was in Brazil, in Foz do Iguaçu, training some of our customers when my sister phoned me and said, "Our mother passed away last night. Where are you?"

"Oh no," I said. "She had a beautiful life, but it is still hard to hear this. When is the funeral?"

"It will be tomorrow afternoon, you know in Portugal we cannot wait," Luisa said.

"Okay, I will let you know if I can come."

I immediately phoned the travel agency and got a same-day flight to Lisbon arriving the next morning.

I had to buy a black suit and tie locally as she was going to be buried the same day I arrived. In Portugal, it is mandatory to bury people within a very short time. There were many people there, family and friends I had not seen for decades, even distant family and friends of my mother, who came from very far away. It was an interesting trip, even if it was very sad because of my mother. She had passed away at ninety-eight years old and in full health. She just went to bed and never woke up again. I do not think you can top that.

One of the last things my mother told my sister was, "Give my mink coat to your brother." At the time I did not understand it, but now I know that it was confirmation that she knew and accepted me for who I am.

Back in Florida, I was working like crazy. I was traveling a lot, now mostly to Europe and Israel to sort out a problem with an old customer I used to be the key account manager for. During the time that I was not dealing with this account, the customer stopped all the deliveries because of a technical problem. I was called in because I knew the customer very well, and together with our factory in Ramat HaSharon, near Tel Aviv, I was going to sort out the technical issues.

The CEO of that plant, the person who brought me to the U.S., was very active in finding the cause and prescribing solutions. He did a great job. After a lot of work we managed to detect the causes, convince the customer, and renegotiate the contract. During this negotiation, I was either in northern Germany, Israel, or Florida. We were nearing the end of the negotiation with the customer, and only the final signatures were missing. The contract content was already clear, when some drastic changes took place.

I suddenly got an internal e-mail from headquarters with the people that had been fired in the U.S., and guess what? Yep. My name was there, too. It was September 2013. I was living in the U.S. on a work visa; I had applied for my green card, but it had not arrived. My wife and I were scared that we would have to go back to Europe. This was completely unexpected and came as quite a large shock.

My departure negotiation with VR was long and difficult. They did not give me much money, just enough to get started. Fortunately for me I had negotiated a good contract, so I could stay at least another six months in Florida to wait for my papers. By the end of October of the same year, Karin and I got our green cards, and that opened the doors to a completely new life for us.

Unfortunately for VR, the impact of me leaving the company was very clear. In their year-end statement, they lost a large customer and had other tremendous losses. My friend, the CEO of the company in Israel and the Americas, gave his resignation shortly after I left. He immediately started as COO of a new company.

The loss of knowhow and good people, and I am not only talking about myself, was disastrous to VR. They continue to lose money every year, many, many millions; they're lucky that the owner has not cut them yet. The CEO of the company that fired me was then fired in 2016. He was at the company just over three years and created something like a 173 million CHF loss during his stay. For a company that made 345 million in net sales in 2015, this was about half of the net sales we made in 2008. And he was very well paid to do this damage!

While I was looking for a new job, I changed some of my information on LinkedIn, and an old friend sent me a message: "Congratulations on your new job!"

I answered, "Sorry, I have no new job but if you need someone in the USA, let me know."

The answer was, "Well, we do need someone, but we are looking for an agent, not an employee."

Why not? I thought. I have enough money to start my own company, and it could be a very lucrative thing. My advantages are that I know the customers, I know the trade, I know the machines, and mostly I am very good at the applications.

Sometimes you must follow your intuition, hope for the best, and never give up. You have to trust in yourself and pursue what you think is right and true. I have always done that in my life and that was why I succeeded.

The only thing that I always left behind? Well, it was myself.

It was a little risky of course because I would be alone with no real company behind me, but in December of the year that I left VR, I started my own company, FFM Industrial Solutions LLC, a Florida-based company. 2014 was a very hardworking year for me, getting my company established, getting other suppliers and customers, but by the end of that year, I got my first large order.

I built everything from the ground up, from the website to accounting, traveling to customer visits and making sales, to get the business going. Unfortunately with the fall of oil prices, the mining industry, oil, gas, and all the mills had no work, so my chances of selling something got very small. I was just doing the minimum. Probably a blessing in disguise.

By the beginning of 2015, I had time to think and feel, and, as my therapist says, addiction loves a vacuum. I was smoking two packs of cigarettes per day and doing everything like an addict: working too much, gaming, eating ... I was getting into a real depression; I knew I was not happy. It got so bad that I decided to see a therapist, and I found someone that could help me: Dr. Carol Clark in Miami.

It was not long after I started talking to her that we got into my issues and feelings and found out what was wrong. I was transgender, and she officially diagnosed me with Gender Dysphoria on June 30, 2015, after many months of counseling.

My new life started on July 30 when I began hormone replacement therapy. Things started to get clear. I stopped smoking, lost fifty pounds, and started a new life. It was the end of fifty-five years of suffering and playing the cross-dresser that I was in men's clothes.

2015 was slow for business, but at year's end, I received some good news that investments by very large companies had started to come forward. I had to wait another eight months until mid-2016 to receive the large purchase orders, but it was a start for FFM.

With that behind me, my big worry is of course my transition as it relates to my business, something that will come very soon and will be a real challenge. Courage and integrity are the keywords.

Conclusion

"It's more fun to arrive a conclusion than
to justify it."

Malcolm Forbes

As a transgender woman, I have been blessed all
my life. Not because I embraced this cause early.
Like many of us, I was one of the victims of a
society that does not know how to cope with trans
people. I was blessed because I have had a great
life, a great family, and I managed to create a life
that is positive and constructive.

On the other hand, being closet transgender most
of the time led to a life of running alone from place
to place and hiding my feelings, and I must say I
ran from myself for most of my life. I suffered a lot
because I was afraid of my feelings, because I was

made to feel guilty from an early age, and this followed me all my life.

Yes, I was blessed, though, because compared to most transgender people, I was one of the ones that had a good life, full of acceptance and positive experiences. But the price I had to pay was to forget and bottle up my feelings for sixty years. I escaped by being a workaholic, traveling from place to place to find new people and experiences, and to be isolated from myself. Why didn't I have the opportunity to have a good life and be my true self?

Yes, my fears and guilt played a big role, and this is something I don't want future generations of transgender people to experience. I know I am not the only one to have such experiences and life.

Although this book is about me, it is meant as an example for a community that is mostly suffering. Many must go through a lot of negativity, discrimination, and violence to become who they really are, and unfortunately many never get there.

We should not forget that transgender people suffer, even today when a lot of progress has been made, thanks to some iconic pioneers. Lack of acceptance, hardship, harassment, and discrimination are still an everyday reality at any age of transition. And we will see what politics bring to our community in the next few years.

The list of famous transgender people that has increased awareness for us is getting bigger and bigger by the day. Today we talk about people like Caitlyn Jenner, Jazz Jennings, Laverne Cox, Chaz Bono, Carmen Carrera, and please excuse me if I did not mention all of you. We are many, and we are invincible.

National Geographic just published a special issue on the gender revolution. To see a real reference publication discuss this really shows the world the degree of our acceptance. Yes, finally, transgender people are seen as people and not as dirt, but this is still very different, depending on the geographical location.

But let us look at our history. *Transgender* is a very modern term for a group of people that always existed and had to suffer for many centuries because of the puritanical societies in many parts of the world.

On the North American continent, the Native Americans had the so-called "two spirits" that were recorded in more than 130 tribes. Two Spirits have been reported by the Spanish conquistadores, and by missionaries as far back as the beginning of the eighteenth century. Their presence was described as a fundamental institution among most tribes, and they were respected. They were integrated into the social and functional life of the tribes and would go to war as well. Like transgender people today, and according to Sabine Lang, a German anthropologist, "The mere fact that a male wears women's clothing does not say something about his role behavior, his gender status, or even his choice of partner." This is still true today.

As far back as 4,000 years ago, in the old Assyrian Empire which is the Middle East today, there were already reports of transgender people. Some were in cults as priestesses, some took part in public processions, singing and dancing, and some were prostitutes. Around 630 BC, King Ashurbanipal, a remarkable person that left us the oldest-surviving library in the world, spent most of his (or her) life presenting as a female in traditional female clothing. Earlier, in Egypt around 1470 BC, Queen Hatshepsut, the third female pharaoh in 3,000 years, was reported to wear traditional male clothes and even wore a beard like most pharaohs. Around 855 AD, one of the first popes, John Anglicus, was born a woman later known as Pope Joan. It is said that no one in the Catholic world knew until he gave birth during a papal procession.

I was born a boy, from Venus

In South Asia, mostly India and Pakistan, the Hijra is an ancient caste of transgender people that the Indian supreme court legally recognized together with other transgender people as the third sex in 2014. This caste is mentioned in the Kama Sutra, and is mentioned with many Indian gods like its patron, the Lord Shiva, and Bahuchara Mata. Under British Imperial rule, between 1858 and 1947, there was an attempt to eradicate them. There were anti-Hijra laws that described them as a criminal tribe. This was a terrible time for all of India, but like the Indian people, the Hijra caste has survived the test of time.

Transgender people were also known in ancient Persia. They were part of many old classical civilizations such as the Greek and Roman empires.

Throughout modern history there were some transgender personalities that became famous such as: the Chevalier d'Éon, a famous French transgender woman, spy, and diplomat born in 1728 as a man. Albert Cashier, a trans man in the American Civil War who fought in over forty battles. Michael Dillon, the first trans man to undergo a sex reassignment surgery, was born in 1915. He was a very famous British physician and did extensive work on endocrinology and ethics.

I was born a boy, from Venus

The French Crusader Jean d'Arc or Joan of Arc was born as woman but always wore men's clothes. It is not clear if she was a cross-dresser or had a male gender identity. Lucy Hicks Anderson, born in 1886, was a black trans woman and lived as a woman; she was jailed many times for fraud. Anderson is considered the earliest pioneer for marriage equality. Born in Denmark in 1882, Lili Elbe was the first trans woman to have a sex reassignment surgery. She was a lesbian as well, and a recent great film, *The Danish Girl*, has been made about her. These are just to mention a few; there are considerably more examples throughout history.

I have always wanted to meet transgender people, near my home and on my travels. Transgender people are not easy to find for many reasons: first, we are a minority, probably less than one percent of the global population. Second, as per definition they are transitioning, so they are in many different stages. Some trans women and trans men cannot be distinguished anymore from other men or women because they are at the end stage of their transition, and many of these do not need or want to identify as transgender people.

Unfortunately, many transgender women are forced to become prostitutes or do sex work to survive. I saw many of those people, starting in France in the "Bois de Boulogne" in the 80's and 90's, in street prostitution in Italy, some on the same street as one of the factories I worked for. But for trans women, prostitution also exists in Switzerland, India, and in many other countries. I always felt sad for these women; it always reminded me that it could have been me. Some of these girls are very beautiful. Many have had many operations and had no signs of masculinity whatsoever.

I still pray for these women. Society always has had issues with transgender people, both men and women; they were never respected or treated like human beings. Two thousand, two hundred and sixty transgender people were murdered between 2008 and mid-2016 because of hate crimes. The most affected people are of course sex workers. The largest murdered population comes from Brazil and South, Central, and North America, mainly from the Latin countries.

The transgender community is a small amount of the population. In the U.S. it is believed that about 1.4 million people openly identify as such, so the actual statistic is probably twice that, considering the people that have not came out as transgender. The statistics published by the National Center for

Transgender Equality are quite clear. It is hard to believe that in many countries, criminals that attack, rape, or even murder transgender people will not be prosecuted. Our lives do not matter in those countries. Suicide, sexual violence, harassment, homelessness, and bullying are very widespread with the transgender community.

Why are transgender people the victims of harassment or violence? The statistics are unbelievable:

46% of transgender persons were verbally harassed.

9% of transgender people were physically attacked in the last year alone

47% of transgender people were sexually assaulted at some point in their lifetime.

54% have experienced some type of partner violence.

This is so much higher than the general population.

We dream of a world where one is accepted as one is, meaning regardless of color, religion, gender, sexual orientation, and where there is love for all of us, transgender or not. Where you can go out and not have the fear of being harassed or violated.

I was born a boy, from Venus

And for the U.S., I must state, I dream of a country where I can use the bathroom I belong to, regardless of my appearance, in peace, without the fear of going to jail or paying a fine.

I have attended several transgender support groups in the past, and I've heard a similar story many times. Most transgender people knew that they were in the wrong body at an early age. The things that make the biggest difference are the amount of family support, the support of their social environment, and the age at which they transitioned. People that transitioned later in life were usually confronted with no acceptance when they were young. Some were strong enough to follow their feelings and transition, but many, myself included, tried to escape from our own reality and show openly that they conformed with the way they were born for a long time. Many would even go to extremes and would join the military, the police, do extreme sports and other things to express the extremities of their masculinity. This also happens with trans men conforming to feminine gender norms. But many others broke down and turned to drugs, alcohol, or other addictions. Is this fair? What can society do to help them?

I was born a boy, from Venus

Some of us are lucky enough to be recognized and accepted by our families at an early age, but their challenges are high as well; society is not always kind, and we are still in early days as far as infrastructure and acceptance are concerned. And the social hurdles of getting to stability are many. Here I think of some of the issues that Jazz Jennings has gone through at puberty, just for one example.

I know this book has concentrated more on trans women, but I want to emphasize that trans men go through the same issues, and I love and admire my transman friends. Many are very cool and handsome.

Support of transgender people by their families and their environment is so important! With cis people, learning and roleplaying with gender norms takes place early in life and is something normal and expected.

With transgender people, the degree of self-confidence is mostly not very high in the beginning because they are learning to live in their real gender and accept social rules for that gender when they are much older, and have already undergone some training for the gender of birth. If on top of this learning, there is a complete rejection by family and society, many extreme reactions can be expected like suicide, addiction, and more.

Society has changed so incredibly fast in my lifetime. Until the 1970s, only a couple of transgender people would dare to show who they were. In most western countries, transgender people would be arrested for fraud; very often, the only work they could do was sex work. In the East, there were communities for us, and transgender people could have household work or other types of care-related work.

In the 1980s, some transgender pioneers appeared, and people started to talk about us. The acceptance in the U.S. just in the last two years has been tremendous, and a real game-changer. Action and reaction always come together, and in some places, laws against our community have been made, mainly concerning bathrooms, which is a real shame. We will see what happens next, but I can foresee some real challenges coming.

I must say that living in South Florida now for over one full year as woman has been a beautiful experience. Most people accept me as I am without much fuss. Mostly women are open and friendly; some men are very nice, opening doors for me. Only on the rarest occasions do I have some people that are negative towards me or show a small degree of harassment. Even in most places, people do not stare or act impolite, and that to all levels of transition. This is the local experience of course; it is not said that the rest of the country, or even the world, is the same way, and again, I do believe that I am very privileged. One still has to be very careful; I do know transgender people that have been raped, violated, or harassed in this area as well.

My evolution as a transgender person was not simple or easy. It started by being punished because I was wearing clothes that I felt good in. That drove me into long decades of hiding from the world. I developed a very painful routine of going into a room and getting in my own little feminine world to feel peaceful and happy. I was in a magical world, that is, until those moments were finished, and I felt guilty for having done so. If those feelings stopped because I fell asleep, or the dream period naturally ended, it was more or less acceptable and I carried on. But if this awakening was forced, like if I got caught, then a deep knife of guilt entered my heart.

Later, when I started to accept myself, there was still this moment of difficulty, because I wanted to blend in when I went out as my real self. It was difficult because I was not so perfect in my new role, and I was very insecure. My feelings had changed from guilt to insecurity.

Whenever I would go to a shop or out on the street, my mind would tell me that everyone was looking and making fun of me, but this was only my mind creating these things due to a long-standing foundation of guilt. Most people do not care or even look at you. The ones that look? Some notice, but most don't, depending on the degree of perfection you have achieved and their perceptive abilities. And then the ones who look may give you a comment, not because you are transgender, but because they are giving you a compliment, or commenting on something specific about you. Some things you must get used to. For me it was the fact that some men tried to comment on the way I looked or pick me up as a girl. It is flattering, but for me still unusual, clearly part of the new role. One can get used to it, if it is positive.

As an example, say you are walking down the street and see two men laughing. In the beginning, I thought they were laughing because of me, the way I looked, the way I talked, but that was my guilty feeling rising up. Most likely, they were just telling jokes or laughing for some other reason. Of course, a similar situation could be about you, but

I was born a boy, from Venus

I am sure you would notice it more clearly if that was truly the case.

I do believe that we are going in the right direction, as far as acceptance is concerned, but it will take some time.

The role of the family, partnerships, and the acceptance of parents and siblings is so important. The younger this acceptance comes, the better. When the guilty feeling I have described does not exist for a young person, we start to identify with the real gender we feel. As a result, growth is easier both on the physical and psychological side.

When I was small, in the 50's, the typical attitude from my family was: "Dolls are for girls," "Boys don't cry," "Stop taking your sister's clothes; they're not for boys," or "Boys that wear girl's clothes are weird," and of course, the physical punishment if I was caught. There you go, my guilty feeling was building up.

Today in some cases the attitude has changed, but even like that, only a small number of transgender people are strong enough to tell their parents the way they feel in a manner that they can understand. Unfortunately, many things are lost in communication. Siblings are usually more accepting, and sometimes they become partners in crime. But, at any age, the fact of telling your parents and siblings is a real challenge that cannot be neglected; it takes a lot of courage.

For a transgender person, acceptance is so important. First you must accept yourself, and in the beginning, your outer appearance does not match up with how you feel on the inside, and this can be difficult. You are perfecting yourself with no real guarantee of success. Some people are more lucky than others because of the way they look or how old they are. The older a person is before transitioning, the more difficulty they will have to look passable as their true gender. When we are transitioning, we are looking for help to become more passable and nice, and if at this stage what you get are negative feelings, it may lead to disaster. Acceptance from others is so important because you do not want to become lonely, that is, until you find out you are not the only one like this. Thank God for the Internet! There is a massive amount of information available for all of us, and depending on the region, there are support groups and clubs that can help you.

Love from your friends, siblings, and close family is very important, but if you have a life partner, the challenges climb to another level. In my case, my partner knew that I was transgender from the day I met her, but did she really understand it? We do not want to hurt people, but we need to be what we are, and a refusal from the partner is very hurtful to us.

Some transgender partnerships stay together, but it is a real challenge. Is it sometimes necessary to keep something alive that is not necessarily there anymore? The guilty feeling in such cases, if there is a refusal or denial from one's partner, is immense and unfair because both partners come from a point that is natural to them. The transgender person wants to unite his or her looks with the way he or she feels, and the other partner wants to have a conventional partnership – the same one they always thought they had. Both feelings are correct, but both have to go through some kind of compromise for the partnership to continue, and that is not easy. I believe that, if a compromise can be found, the partnership will be stronger and better than ever, but if this is not the case, people should take a next step and each be happy in their different directions.

A partnership with a transgender person can have its advantages. It is a deep personal relationship with a person who often has similar tastes and habits. One important point as well is that transgender people change their appearance and the way they behave, but inside they are the same people as before. Very often the development is not so extreme as one might think.

It is interesting, for a while after my transition, I loved to go shopping and to get my nails done with my ex-spouse and my family. We had quite an intensive social life, doing many things I would not do before. One of the greatest compliments I ever got was from my daughter, who said in one of the transgender groups: "Before the transition, my daddy used to sit in his corner in the garden, smoke and drink incredibly, no interaction with the family. Since he transitioned, he is part of the family, we do many things together. He stopped smoking and almost never drinks. We can talk and understand each other." This is the kind of positive change you get when you go through the hurdles and work on becoming yourself and at peace with yourself. Well our marriage did not survived and we divorced some years later. We did had a great time together but it was time for each one of us to carry on their journeys.

But by far the sexual challenge is the greatest in a transitioning partnership. Many trans women and trans men want go through sex reassignment surgery. Is that still appealing to your partner? What about the effects of hormone replacement therapy on your sex life? It's not necessarily the same for all, but it's certainly a challenge.

Yes, transgender people have to live, too, and most are not born into wealth. We are very thankful that so many companies in this day and age are transgender-friendly and actively support our cause, simply by accepting us as their workers. The intellectual level of transgender people is widespread. Some are scientists, bankers, engineers, police officers, social workers, doctors, you name it. It is not surprising that many transgender people are in the army, and today they are accepted there, too, to the point of getting quite a lot of treatments from the military itself.

All this evolution in acceptance in the last decades is very positive, but let us not forget that many transgender people have to do sex work to survive. I know of one that told me, "When my family understood that I was transgender, they told me I had to survive by myself. They were not going to do anything for me." So this trans man became a porn star, a female porn star, because at the time the porno industry did not want to deal with transgender people.

Even today, many transgender people are fired for the simple reason that they want to be their real selves. Yes, transphobia is still a real threat in the workplace, and transgender people are still not protected in most states and countries in the world. Many companies are simply unable to cope when one of their workers tells them who they are. Today there are some consulting companies that specialize in transgender HR and organization in the workplace. Another big step for acceptance.

One aspect that is very important for good integration is how we present ourselves. If you are MTF transgender, you behave like a woman or a girl. There are many manners that have to be learned properly, like using a more feminine voice and feminine words, the way one walks, sits, gets in the car, and many others. A good example is trans women that cannot close their legs properly while wearing a skirt. The way you look is very important as well. Your chances of getting a job are often proportional to the level of how you present yourself to others. But let us be realistic: even with cis women, it is the same thing.

If you are FTM, the challenges are very high as well. In the beginning, most trans men must hide their breasts, and that can be a painful challenge. Here, too, their appearance and the way they talk and present themselves is important. When they start to be very passable in the work environment, they still must deal with cis men that are very hostile towards women. This may hurt them quite strongly in a business sense.

The role of plastic surgery for both trans men and trans women is very important in integrating into a new role easily. In any case, if you are MTF or FTM, you have to walk the walk and talk the talk of your new gender in order to be accepted, and that takes time, money, and a lot of patience.

I was brought up Catholic, and from a very young age I had access to the Jewish faith, so I was always interested in different religions. I was able to develop this interest through my different travels, mainly in India. At a young age, I was a Boy Scout and learned that God loved all creatures, no matter what type, race, gender, status, or income.

Well, the reality seems to be very different from the teachings. Many churches do not accept transgender people, at least not officially, like they do not accept LGBT. Hell, some religions do not even accept divorce. What kind of hypocrites can renounce the state of their own followers? Why do they have to tell us what is right or wrong when they themselves shelter a lot of abusers of children and society? Why do the same people have to feel that they should send LGBT people to conversion training, where they hope that they will not be gay or transgender anymore? How many suicides happen after such a terrifying experience?

I have a wonderful neighbor that is a very religious person. He lost his wife to cancer last year, and we do not see him every day in Florida because he is a snow bird. Once, while he was at home in Florida, I came to see him dressed as a man to say hi and inform him of my transition. He immediately told me that he was very conservative, but he was also a human being.

The next day, he invited my spouse and me to one of the best restaurants in Boca. I came as Ella. He was kind of shocked but agreeable. We had a great dinner, but he was clear to tell me that I could not come to his church dressed like this. Luckily some religions are more advanced than others and not all abuse us with extremes such as violence, intolerance, or hate. There are good examples of individual churches within a religion that are actively tolerant and receive us with open arms and support. Sometimes, though, they are not highly regarded by their own top hierarchy.

I remember as well that when I was small, I thought I would like to become a priest because they had dresses, and they did not have to get married. Then I found out that this was a motivation for many gay men to become priests back then, which was something I did not identify with.

I sincerely believe in God, but I do not know what his or her real name is: Krishna, Allah, Christ, Shiva (who is half-male and half-female, by the way), Baha'i, or Buddha. I believe less in religions that are fully or partly intolerant. They are old-fashioned, sometimes with medieval ideas, and do not represent the values of the society they represent. I must say, though, that I pray every day and believe very strongly that I have an ongoing discussion with God.

The position of transgender people worldwide has changed so much in the last few years. The global impact of shows like *I am Jazz* or *I am Cait* is enormous for our community. People are starting to become aware of us, and many admire our courage for admitting and following who we really are.

Unfortunately, in this political arena, both sides are represented, the friends and the fiends. We have to fight for our rights because things are not automatically accepted, especially now with the new political evolution in the U.S. and worldwide that open the doors to transphobia. Bathroom rights are just one fight that hurts people; in some places and countries we have gone back to the times of Apartheid or Jim Crow Laws, only this time it is with us, the transgender people.

Well, the transgender version of the green book, where transgender people can find safe bathrooms, already exists as an app. In case you do not know what the green book was, it was a travel guide for people of color that was introduced in the 1930s, so that they knew, for every city or state, where to go to the toilet, eat, or go to a hotel where they would be accepted. It was published for over thirty years. Please note that in some hotels in the U.S., transgender people are still not allowed.

Transgender people have a much more difficult fight in other countries and civilizations, like in the Arab world and in Russia, where they are put in prison and suffer physical and mental harassment. In other countries like Brazil they are hunted and killed by anti-transgender squads.

I believe that together with the Human Rights Campaign, the transgender movement must progress and defend transgender people on a global scale. It is by no means the only cause that has to be taken globally. Women, as well as the lesbian and gay communities, still suffer in many parts of the world. How long will all of this last?

I was born a boy, from Venus

Back to our Western world and mostly here in the U.S., courage is a major factor for a good transition, but so is self-confidence and a lot of luck and support within the community. It is so nice to see that today so many transgender people are accepted in society and have the opportunity to be positive examples for others. Some have become important in the banking world, others have become actresses and actors, some politicians; many are lawyers, economists, pilots, and so much more.

I am working to carry on my dream of owning a transgender-friendly company, where I can employ transgender people that are successful and creative in the engineering world.

Yes, God made me perfect as a transgender woman. I am not talking about the way I look, but the fact that there are many genders, and we do not live in a binary world. Yes, transgender are perfect human beings, too, irrespective of the way they look. If they are male to female or female to male, if they are intersex, genderfluid, or whatever their identity may be.

Thank you for reading this book. I would like to close by expressing clearly that being transgender is not an option. It is what we are and the way we feel. It takes courage from our side, a lot of it, as

I was born a boy, from Venus

well as acceptance and compassion from the rest of the world, so please accept us and support our rights.

www.ingramcontent.com/pod-product-compliance
Lightning Source LLC
La Vergne TN
LVHW011347080426
835511LV00005B/162